<u>Management</u>

Golden Nugget Methods to Manage Effectively

Teams, Personnel Management, Management Skills, and Conflict Resolution

Ross Elkins

© Copyright 2015 - All rights reserved.

Ross Elkins

Table of Contents

Introduction

Most of the managers today are equipped with skills to manage their teams. Beyond that, as a manager you need something else to manage your teams effectively, resolve conflicts innovatively and adhere to the deadlines every time. This requires special skills that are either obtained by experience or by learning.

This book reveals time-tested strategies that every manager should learn. You will be reading every situation that happens at your work and a better way of dealing with it. It takes a lot of time for your team to accept you as a leader, but if you are able to pull of something extraordinary that the team and your management expects, you are in for a big game.

This book introduces you to a novel concept of game changing strategies that every manager should adopt in a given situation. Time and again, you are expected to deliver and these expectations never come down. Apart from motivating your team and getting the desired results you too need motivation at a different level. You will learn all these and many more from every chapter that is crafted for the manager and leader in you.

To survive, organizations must deliver value. Private and public organizations face the challenge to be faster, cheaper, better, more reliable, more responsive and more convenient. Success today is no indicator of future success, or even survival.

And to do all the above, you need a team that can deliver everything on time every time. This book provides golden nuggets or chunks of process-oriented methods that can be picked up from any page. You can implement these ideas at any point of time in any given situation.

Chapter 1

Effective Team Management Skills

Teams have the potential of exponentially empowering an organization as every member completes the other and in turn creates synergy. Creating and managing effective teams is a challenge worth taking on as the benefits of synergy are a great reward.

In this chapter you will learn and understand tools and thoughts on how to create and manage effective teams in the workplace. Management theory identifies a team as 3 or more members with the opportunity to create hierarchies and interactions amongst them (therefore a large group of people is not a team). There are three distinct types of teams:

- Organic Growth teams – Teams that are supported by an organizational structure.
- Project Specific teams – Teams that are assembled for a specific project.

- Non-organic Growth teams – Teams that are assembled in an organization for a specific process or task or multi-disciplinary teams.

The role of a manager

In every team the manager plays a role in which professional as well as procedural guidance holds an extremely important place. Effectiveness of teams can be described as effectiveness compared to the target set at the forming of the team or as effectiveness compared to resources. What we look for in effective teams is the synergy. Synergy is what separates a good team from just a team and what enables team based organizations to create a viable competitive advantage over time.

In order to create and manage effective teams, a manager must work to enable the advantages of a team to bloom. A manager of a good effective team must use the following characteristics to most benefit the organization:

- Use the differential knowledge of team members – The sum of knowledge in a team is obviously greater than of any individual. Moreover, differential knowledge creates that sought after synergy. To this extent, a manager must strive to know each of the team members as personally as possible. If the team is too big to be able to know each and every one of the team members personally, the manager should at least strive to develop a good enough relationship with the people he or she identifies as key role players around whom the others can rally. Without a significant enough relationship with team members, a manager can't utilize their strengths to the full and minimize the effects of their weaknesses, both of which are key to maximizing the team's performance.

- Enable diversity of opinion and approach – Different team members have accumulated different experience and to solving problems. Use that resource in order to address issues in a variety of ways. It's important that a manager of a good team is open-minded, humble and secure with him or herself in order to effectively create an atmosphere of freedom of expression of ideas while minimizing tension that may arise out of such. If the manager isn't open-minded or humble, team members won't express their potentially effective and groundbreaking ideas that can further make the team more effective. If the manager isn't secure with him or herself, he or she wouldn't be able to really call the shots according to their better judgment and will always defer or succumb to what his or her subordinates dictate. Being humble and open to the fact that he or she doesn't have all the ideas, the manager has access to more ideas that can help the team become more effective. By being secure with him or herself, the manager is able to truly weed out and implement what he or she feels are the best ideas regardless of the team members opinion.
- Acceptance and commitment – Being a part of a process or team creates acceptance and commitment to the team and to its goals. To this extent, a manager of an effective team should be able to foster great relationships not just between him or her and each team member but also among each and every team member. Although it's practically impossible to make each and every team member BFFs (best friends forever) with each other, it is

possible to facilitate a deep enough relationship that fosters a sense of commitment to and acceptance of the team as a whole and of each other. It's been said that 3 strands of cord can't easily be torn and by fostering such a relationship among team members, a manager is able to make a strong team of "3 strands of cords". The stronger the team is, the more effective it can be. As such, the manager should encourage the team to share and make use of every team member in order to create that commitment.

- Offer team members a stage to show intellectual abilities – A manager of an effective team should regularly provide team members with gradually increasing work challenges because it's an opportunity to both showcase and further improve their abilities and strengths. A team member with the great ability to solve problems won't flourish for the team's benefit if he or she isn't given assignments that involve fixing problems. If that team member is assigned to procedural and clerical work that's routinely, that team member's abilities will stagnate, morale will sag and the team won't be able to maximize that person's strength. Team members will flourish if given the opportunity to express themselves through their skills and abilities because it will make them feel affirmed, empowered and confident.

- Do not be afraid of disputes – Disputes lead to growth in a team. A manager of a good team is able to handle disputes among team members very well knowing that such disputes can be good opportunities to make the team even better. Disputes can be looked at either as a "problem" or an opportunity to fill in a weakness, which leads to a much stronger team. If the manager isn't afraid of disputes, he or she is able to use those for the team's advantage.

Manager and the effective team

A manager of a good effective team must also be wary of the following unwanted characteristics of teams:

- Avoid group pressure – A manager of a good and effective team should be first and foremost the leader of the team. If he or she is able to assert his or her leadership well, the chances of one or more team members dominating the team and the risk of group pressure will be minimal if not neutralized. Group pressure effects free thought and expression subduing great possible ideas. As such, a manager should develop his or her leadership skills in order to minimize group pressure and dominance of certain members. Remember, a manager needs every team member to be comfortable expressing his or her opinions and ideas if he or she wants to maximize the team's performance.

- Do not let one member take control over a team. As mentioned earlier, a manager should be able to take control of a team in order to minimize or prevent group pressure or dominance by any single member. A good leader is one that knows when to be gracious and when to put his or her foot down. A good leader is both encouraging, inspiring and respected and as such, the risk of a member controlling the team is virtually nil.

- Politics should be avoided – Do not enable politics between team members. Compromises made using political power harm the team's goals and effectiveness, as they might not be the optimum outcome of a team. This is one of the reasons why a manager should be able to foster good relationships among his or her team members. The better the relationships among the members are, the less opportunities and "need" for politics and gossip. Again, there's no perfect team with perfect relationships but it is possible to foster great enough relationships within the team that can minimize or even neutralize politics and gossiping. And aside from the ability to foster relationships, another thing a manager should be able to do is discourage politics and gossiping about each other either through positive or negative reinforcement.

- Keep the original goals of the team at the center – Consider the target-shooting booth at most carnivals and fairs. Have you ever tried shooting the targets with a rifle whose barrel is very slightly bent just by a few degrees? I have and believe me, even just a one-degree misalignment of the barrel can lead to missing the target by a mile. It's the same with a team's goals, which should be the focus of all the team's efforts. It's easier said than done, especially in the midst of too many "activities" that many times seem to be related to goals but are actually causing the team to slowly drift away. If not consciously managed, the team may eventually be rendered ineffective in light of its original goals.

- Avoid groupthink – Groupthink is a word used to describe a phenomenon where team decisions are based on consensus. Now, group thinking per se isn't wise or unwise in and by itself but making it the primary way of deciding a team's courses of action is unwise. This happens in teams where the leader prioritizes harmony among the team members or tries to free him or herself from the responsibility of having to make the decision (and escape blame if the decision bombs) instead of focusing on what's best for the team and its original goals. This is definitely one of the most dangerous characteristics of teams and should be avoided or minimized at all costs. Group thinking, as a primary basis for making team decisions, usually leads to unwanted solutions and can severely harm an organization. Developing strong leadership skills for the manager and ensuring team members aren't very homogenous, i.e., very similar in backgrounds and personalities, are keys to minimizing the risk for this.

Utilizing the tools mentioned above will help create synergy in a team as a result of mutual fertilization of ideas. This process is as intuitive as it might be analytical. A manager of a good and effective team must learn how scientific an intuitive art of synthesizing team members' strengths and ideas and use the synthesized results to steer the team to success.

To do this, managers must recognize that they play a central role in effective team building. To be successful however, managers need a framework to guide their activities. As a manager you'll need considerable planning and knowledge of the environment in which your team operates to implement the strategies for team success that are discussed below.

Identify team characteristics before you say "go"

The success of team-building efforts is a function of the number of desirable team characteristics that can be built into a work environment. The actual mix of factors considered relevant is a function of the type of team being formed (e.g., temporary vs.

Ross Elkins

permanent), tasks performed, the team's level in the organization, the length of time it has been in existence, and the ease of substitutability of existing members.

When forming a new temporary team, the manager is normally interested in the technical and interpersonal skills of potential members that are relevant to the group's tasks, the power distribution of selected members, and whether or not selected members adequately represent relevant constituencies. The key to creating an effective new, temporary team is balance in the attributes of team members, and the presence of needed resources to achieve stated goals. That's why it was noted earlier that as a manager of an effectively good team, you should be able to know your team members – the key ones at least, if it's impractical to know all members personally. Without such knowledge, you really can't balance each team member's personalities and strengths for optimum team performance. For this, you'll need good relationship skills. Not perfect, but good ones.

For example, in problem solving and implementation teams, managers must make sure that critical managers with powerful personalities and strong ability to implement programs and strategies are selected as members. With a powerful personality, such key members won't be easily swayed by peer pressure won't be concerned with pleasing the people they are supervising. Therefore, when decisions are made, non-participating managers cannot easily resist. Similarly, managers want to ensure that the required expertise and knowledge exists within the group and delegating key tasks to people with strong abilities for program implementation makes that possible and consequently, lowers the risk for failed team strategies.

This increases the probability of creative problem solving and outcome acceptance by non-members. It may be different for more established groups, however. In the case of intact groups, where the work unit already exists, management is likely to consider a different set of factors, particularly set mindsets. This happens because members of intact groups usually don't sit well with inter-group transfer because they're already comfortable being engaged in their current tasks, which are already well established. It's human nature to be risk averse and being transferred out of one's comfort zone is, for many people, considered risky because having to adapt to new responsibilities outside of their comfort zone may entail some level of failure in the beginning as well as more effort when adapting.

Consequently, when intact groups are not achieving desired synergies, it is the managers responsibility to identify' those team characteristics likely to have a positive impact on team behavior and change the existing climate so as to remove existing deficiencies. Again, knowing team members' well, especially their strengths, weaknesses and what makes them tick is the key to be able to adjust accordingly to foster an environment conducive for desired synergies.

Creating a team profile from the characteristics identified

Once a manager is able to identify the team's positive characteristics, he or she must be able to wisely utilize such characteristics for maximum performance by clearly linking these characteristics together. As such, managers must find a way to measure the degree to which relevant team characteristics currently exist in a given environment. There are basically three traditional approaches to collecting this information: paper-and pencil questionnaires or surveys, direct observation and interviews.

Questionnaire method – the paper and pencil

One of the oldest and still most popular methods, paper and pencil questionnaires allow managers to assess the perceptions of group members. Unfortunately, they require significant time to develop because for the participants to honestly answer the questions, they must comfortable enough with whoever is conducting the survey. This requires a certain relationship level and this takes some time and effort.

Another concern with this method is that it normally doesn't allow for real-time clarification by the individuals who complete them or follow-up questions by the manager using them. To remedy this, the concerned manager should be around when the questionnaires are being answered.

Direct observation – team and behavior

Direct observation is a second proven technique that can be useful in assessing an existing group or team climate. It requires managers to spend extended periods of time observing, recording, and assessing pre-identified behavioral dimensions and support behaviors. There can be no other way.

It is assumed that the observer knows specifically what he or she is looking for and is skilled in observing and recording employee behaviors, In the case of team performance in an intact group, it requires that managers have been identified. While this technique can be effective, it does have its disadvantages.

One of the primary disadvantages is that direct observation is labor intensive. To effectively assess an existing team climate can require weeks of observation. Because of the tendency for subjects being observed to put their best foot forward, directly observing the team for a day or two may lead to inaccurate assessments and conclusions based on "show" performances. Consistent with statistical principles, the larger the sample size, i.e., number of observation days in this case, the better the assessment or estimate will be. Team members will eventually revert to their natural work habits and characteristics because pretending to be something they're not is impossible to sustain over extended periods of time and circumstances will eventually reveal the true characteristics of the team.

One way to shorten the period of time for direct observation while ensuring that what is observed is the "real" characteristics of the team, you can covertly observe by using a hidden camera. This, however, will cost you and your team quite a bit in terms of money and potentially, integrity if the members find out you're secretly observing them.

Interviewing techniques

A potential compromise between a paper-and-pencil questionnaire and direct observation is the interview. Interviews allow managers to directly interact with group members, respond to non-verbal cues, and ask follow-up questions should the need arise.

Interviews can also be used to supplement information obtained through questionnaires and direct observation. Interviews are most effective if they are well designed, structured, and ask the same question of each participant. It will also help greatly if the manager conducting the interview is relatively well versed in reading body language and is good at drawing out the real answers from the subjects.

As with the questionnaires, having good relationships – or at least giving a good first impression – with the interview subjects will go a long way in helping draw out accurate information during the interview. If they don't perceive you as someone trustworthy and who won't be using the information obtained against them, they won't be totally forthcoming with you and as such, you may not be able to draw out the answers you really need.

Chapter 2

Grooming Team Members and Developing Skills

Now that you've identified your team's characteristics, it's time to build the team up from it. As with athletes preparing well prior to actual competition, you should also prepare your team for it to perform effectively well. There are lot of ways you can groom your teams and develop their skills for your current projects and future prospects.

In order to understand what skills need to be developed you need to first understand what your teams are lacking and then look at those skills to be developed. You're able to do that through the team profiling strategies enumerated in the latter part of the previous chapter. Below are some carefully chosen strategies that you may adopt for grooming and developing your teams based on current situations and environments.

Identify teams that lack in team characteristics

Divide your teams into two – those that have the necessary characteristics on the right side and those that lack them on the left side. You can use a pen and paper or a computer spreadsheet to do this. Teams with profiles that fall to the right are likely to be more effective than teams whose profiles fall to the left. Doing this helps you identify which teams to focus more grooming and development efforts on. When considering team-building interventions, managers should be primarily concerned with poor performing groups whose profile falls on the left side because let's face it, why waste developmental and intervening resources on teams that already have a higher chance of performing well?

Poor team performance may be caused by a misalignment between members' skills and task requirements, lack of training, lack of practice, or the lack of appropriate tools and equipment. The smaller the gap or misalignment, the more effective a team can become. As a manager, it is your responsibility to identify what is lacking in the team and then focus on those aspects till the entire team overcomes it. To this extent, it may be helpful to consult with others who have extensive experience with such activities if ever you feel stuck or unable to effectively identify and fill in such gaps. There's no shame in asking for help. To the contrary, doing so increases your chances of improving team performance.

Opting for right decisions for teams lacking in certain areas

Given the complexity and uniqueness of most business environments, and the interrelationships between team characteristics, it would be administratively unsound to attempt a broad-based intervention without considering how best to proceed.

In other words: which deficiencies should be addressed first and what would be the appropriate sequence of subsequent interventions? Managers should therefore develop and consider a number of decision criteria that would help them address the issues of setting priorities and sequencing.

It's also important that the manager is able to identify the real limiting factors to address in order to make certain teams more effective. For example, if a team is performing poorly in terms of production, you as manager should be able to identify the real problem that's keeping it from consistently meeting production targets. Let me illustrate through a practical example.

Let's say your looking at a team whose function is to assemble 100 units of an electronic gadget daily and is only able to assemble 80 with the following details:

- The assembly process requires 3 phases;

- The 1st phase is handled by a sub-team of 11 people that can handle a maximum of 110 units daily;

- The 2nd phase is handled by a sub-team of 10 people that can handle a maximum of only 90 units daily; and

- The 3rd phase is handled by a sub-team of 5 people that can handle a maximum of 95 units daily.

It's clear that the problems lie with the 2nd and 3rd phases sub-teams but which of the 2 should be given more priority? It should be 3rd phase because even if you address the capacity of the 2nd phase, it will still bottleneck at the 3rd phase. By focusing on the capacity of the 3rd phase first, you'll put the 2nd phase sub-team in a position to effectively increase capacity and make a difference.

However, several examples will help clarify how managers might use relevant criteria to guide their actions. When working on these criteria, managers should already have a detailed understanding of their environments.

First, they need to understand the strengths, weaknesses, interests, and workload of their staff, in particular those who belong to sub-performance teams. If not, it would be impossible to maximize performance because the manager may hire more people and increase operating cost if they aren't aware that the current manpower can still take on additional load. Consequently, the manager may fail to improve team performance by not bringing in new people by overestimating the current team members' ability to take on more responsibilities.

Next, they should be aware of the history, traditions, and existing culture within the company. These psychological factors play a great role in either motivating or de-motivating team members and influencing their attitudes. It's been said that it's the attitude that determines altitude and that a person's "I will" is more important than his or her "I can" and as such, being aware of these important psychological factors can help a manager influence and motivate members of sub-performance teams to do better.

Similarly, they need to know what resources are available and how power is distributed within the organization in the event that they need to get more. Even if a manager knows exactly what makes his staff tick and work, ignorance of available or unavailable resources will directly impact the ability of his or her members to raise the team's performance. If for example, the manager identifies the need for upgrading equipment in order to boost both performance and morale of the team but for some reason, he or she didn't know that there's still available budget for such, the team won't be able to upgrade equipment and thus, continue to perform below par even if the manager has done his or her homework in terms of knowing his or her team's strengths and weaknesses as well as motivating them.

Above all, they must know their own strengths, weaknesses, and aspirations. Mastery of one's self begins with knowing one's self. A manager, thus, should be both self-aware and is comfortable seeking the advice of other people in order to continuously evolve.

In those instances where this information is not at the manager's fingertips, they must take steps to increase their knowledge within the organization. Again, the ability to develop and maintain great working or even personal relationships within and outside the team will come in handy in terms of getting to know the company even more.

Team building strategies

Clearly, the actual team-building strategy, or set of strategies, selected by managers will reflect the unique characteristics of each situation. In other words, managers must have an intimate understanding of the unit and the organization. As a result, it is essential for managers to have what the authors call "Ks" in place. "Ks" refer to an intimate working knowledge of the situation.

Without this working knowledge of their environment, it is unlikely that managers will be able to make correct decisions as to which deficiencies to improve first and in what sequence to address remaining team characteristic deficiencies. It's like trying to drive in an unfamiliar city to get to an unfamiliar address without a map or a GPS device to guide you. The team will just be running around in circles wasting time and resources without such a "K".

There are four data-collection techniques that are capable of providing the necessary "Ks" — real-time observation, review of historical data, interviews, and questionnaires.

The first two are day-to-day data collection techniques that help managers understand their micro and macro environments. TAs such, they are not specific to team building, but rather should reflect the efforts of managers to remain current with their work environments. The "Ks" obtained from these 2 techniques form the base from which team-building strategies will hinged on or built around. The remaining two data collection methods are designed to fine-tune managers' decision-making capabilities when engaging in specific team-building efforts.

For example, if a pencil-and-paper questionnaire is initially used to collect team characteristic data, interviews can be used to thoroughly investigate questions or issues arising from the questionnaire. Similarly, summary scores for each team characteristic may fail to provide the necessary detail assessment of what is occurring in the situation. To ensure that this is not the case, managers can review the sub-dimensions or items used to produce the summary scores.

The 2 sets of data collection techniques complement each other and one technique from each set should be complemented by at least one from the other. Raw data should be processed to yield more specific answers via interviews or questionnaires and the latter 2 won't be possible without any raw data from which to build the questions from.

Identify team building strategies that fill in the gaps

All too often, managers, when attempting to build effective teams, turn to outside professionals to create teams within their units or organization. Once selected, these outside professionals typically take the natural or intact work group off site, and engage in some type of intensive team-building experience.

Carried out in this manner, team-building experiences often take employees away from their jobs for two or three days at a time. There is a reason for this. The assumption is that intact groups or individuals will transfer appropriate team behaviors learned during the team-building sessions back to the job or organizational setting.

While such efforts can sensitize group members to the importance of team characteristics, or kick-start an in-house team-building effort, the usual experience is that desired behaviors often aren't transferred to the work environment. Assuming for the sake of argument that they can be, it's only a matter of time before newly acquired behavior fades away to make way for the old ones. As such, effective team building efforts aren't one-time-big time activities but consist more of the small ones that managers facilitate on a regular basis such as going to lunch every so often as a team or enjoying simple but regular recreational activities outside of work such a watching movies, bowling or karaoke. Compared to team-building activities that have overt rapport-building motives that can put the participants on edge, simpler and more frequent regular bonding activities provide a natural environment for relationships to flourish among team members.

Lastly, as much as the manager plays a key role in facilitating the development of good working relationships among team members through the strong methodologies as explained in this book, he or she can only do so much. Knowing this reality can help managers determine which team characteristic deficiency should be addressed first, identify the sequence of subsequent interventions and articulate the implement the appropriate team-building strategies. In constructing such a list, managers can turn to the team building literature, personal experience, in-house experts or managers, or benchmark best practices in other organizations.

Chapter 3

Teams, Individuals and Conflict Resolution

Conflict in the workplace is inevitable. Managers should also be worried if there are none, even small minor ones. It only means total homogeneity, which as explained earlier, runs the high risk of group thinking.

Conflicts often erupt between people due to different values, personalities, opinions, goals, and needs. The workplace seems to foster differences and value differing viewpoints, which are the exact things that cause conflict to occur.

However, conflict is not always a bad thing. It can lead to innovative solutions that people with similar opinions and viewpoints would not likely achieve. Can you imagine if all members of the team are optimists that eschew any form of caution or planning, which accounts for no conflicts whatsoever? Or how about if all the members of your team are pessimists that are perfectly bonded together by their ability to see the doom and gloom of things? You need a variety of personalities and opinions to be able to exhaust all possible alternatives for the team to be effective.

Since conflicts per se aren't inherently bad, the key to channeling conflict into a positive workplace function is to resolve it effectively. When resolved properly, conflict can cause personal and professional development that leads to employees who are more productive. Conflicts – if handled well – may be considered eustress or positive stress, which is what makes bodybuilders' muscles grow to inhumanly huge proportions. Bodybuilders regularly subject their muscles to a healthy amount (at least for them) stress that causes tiny muscle fiber tears. As these tears heal with proper rest and nutrition, the muscles grow bigger and stronger. Conflicts handled well have the same capacity for building your team's effectivity muscles.

Conflict resolution is necessary in all types of organizations because unresolved ones are potentially dangerous to a team. In most cases, facilitators are assigned the role of helping employees to resolve conflict. Facilitators can be managers, leaders, or designated employees granted the facilitator role in the organization that aren't part of the conflict and are thus, generally perceived by both parties as objective or non-partisan. If not, negotiations or reconciliatory talks won't progress because of one or both parties' lack of trust.

The more educated facilitators are when it comes to resolving conflicts in an effective and healthy way, the better the outcome will be. If you want to be good manager-facilitator for your team, let's take a look at four steps designed to equip you with step-by-step instructions on how to effectively resolve conflict in the workplace.

Meet with the conflicting parties together

This step is one of the most overlooked, yet necessary, steps when employees try to resolve conflict. All parties involved in the conflict should be brought together to discuss the issue at hand. Each party should present its view of the problem without interruptions from the other parties. It is important for each party to hear everyone's viewpoint and to gain a clear picture of why the parties are conflicting with each other.

As a facilitator, you should be able to step in when the other party tries to interrupt and allow the one currently speaking to finish stating their case. You must ensure that each party states its case clearly and calmly without personally attacking the other parties. The more you're able to keep things in order and tempers from escalating, the higher your chances of helping resolve conflicts. On the other hand, your inability to do so increases the risk of reconciliatory talks bogging down.

Seeking suggestions

Ask each party for specific suggestions on how to resolve the conflict. Doing so helps increase the chances of successfully resolving conflicts because by giving both parties the opportunities to recommend a solution, you'll be able to give them a sense of ownership in the resolution of the conflict. It has been observed that having a sense of ownership in solutions to problems increases one's commitment to it because of a sense of accountability and pride knowing that he or she is part of the solution.

Each party should state two to three specific suggestions on how it thinks the conflict could be resolved. For example, "I would like

Sally and Eric to provide me with a project status update by Thursday at 10 a.m., so I can provide an accurate project status update to the client on Friday at 8 a.m."

Another example might be, "I would like to own both new policy requests and claims for my clients to reduce client confusion on who to contact for different requests." These examples are very clear and precise, indicating exactly what actions need to occur and by when in order to resolve the conflict. By giving them several opportunities to do so, you give them more chances of contributing to the actual solution and help make them feel they have a bigger stake in it as well.

As the facilitator, help the parties come up with specific suggestions if either or both parties have a hard time doing so. Try to encourage and help each party identify what action is the root cause of the problem. Once they have done so, prompt them to come up with specific ways that would resolve the issue. Asking additional leading questions to the employees may help trigger the parties to uncover the real underlying problems and not just the symptoms of such. Afterwards, help them to outline a specific course of action to resolve the conflict.

Discuss the issue and agree to make changes

Next, the parties should discuss the suggestions presented in the previous step and agree to make the necessary changes. This step is where each party engages in a negotiation to come up with a resolution plan. Depending on the complexity of the conflict, it may take some time before all parties come to an agreement on what suggestion should be implemented to resolve the conflict.

As the facilitator, ensure that each party is reasonable and professional. Do not allow the parties to be disrespectful to one another or for the discussion to turn into another argument. You must be able to respectfully put your foot down whenever either or both parties start to act or speak in a condescending or offensive manner and nip the potential problem in the bud before it escalates beyond control. As both parties make progress in terms of resolving the conflict, encourage them to give and take in order to make each party feel respected, valued and satisfied with the resolution plan.

Lastly, make sure to remain impartial to either party. Both sides must know that you are there as a neutral party to mediate the conflict. You need the trust and respect of both parties to effectively facilitate the resolution of the conflict and the moment you show partiality, both trust and respect will come flying out the window and destroy the reconciliation process.

Follow-up to ensure that the conflict is resolved

The last step is to set a date for the resolution to be implemented and follow-up on its progress. While all parties might feel better after the creation of a resolution plan in step three, the conflict is not resolved until the resolution plan has been implemented. In fact, failing to follow up on the milestones and timelines set in the resolution plan may lead to another conflict but only this time, it may be more difficult to manage due to unmet expectations and eroded trust. Make sure that the plan is implemented and follow-ups – if needed – be done prior to the date of any particular milestone in order to avoid non-compliance.

Conflict resolution is not an easy job. Actually, it is quite a challenge, even for experienced mediators owing to the fact that mediation isn't an exact science like, say engineering, but more of an art because no two human beings think exactly alike. Facilitators play a key role in helping to maintain a healthy environment for all parties to discuss the problem and reach an agreement to resolve it. Intervening as appropriate can encourage parties to work toward a resolution before the problem gets out of hand. Remember, it's easier to put out a small fire than a raging inferno and timely intervention and conflict resolution is important to make sure that small fire doesn't grow to become a wild one.

In addition, this practice of intervening helps develop your own conflict resolution skills, which is a necessity in today's business world.

Key takes on resolving conflicts

- Conflict is inevitable in the workplace, because companies foster different experiences and viewpoints. As such, it will do you good to expect it and acknowledge it quickly as it arises.

- Conflict is not always a bad thing; healthy conflict can lead to innovative solutions that people with similar opinions and viewpoints would not likely achieve. Conflicts that are resolved in a timely manner may be considered as eustress or good stress that can lead to a much better team, much like weightlifting is important for building bigger and stronger muscles.

- There are four steps that facilitators can follow to resolve conflict in the workplace.

    1. Meet with the conflicting parties together.

2. Ask each party for specific suggestions on how to resolve the conflict.

3. Discuss the issue and agree to make changes.

4. Follow-up to ensure the conflict is resolved.

- Facilitators play a key role in keeping a healthy, balanced environment for all parties to discuss the problem and reach an agreement to resolve it. It is important that facilitators be firm, have a strong enough personality to rein both parties in when they get out of line and objective enough to earn and keep both parties' trust and respect.

Ross Elkins

Chapter 4

Golden Nugget Methods - Proven Techniques

The golden nugget methods for effective management of teams, developing their skills and shaping them are carefully researched ideas that are meant to be useful to you. Understanding and following these will give you an insight of how to manage your teams on a day to basis and ensure that they're groomed and prepared to effectively achieve their goals.

Intervention strategies as part of team building

- Goal Setting (Clarify Behavioral Expectations as to Desired Team Behaviors): Team members have a greater chance of being on the same page when it comes to helping team achieve its goals when they know what is expected of them both individually and collectively. Most conflicts arise due to ambiguity in roles and responsibilities, especially when things go awry and blaming becomes the name of the game. By making individual and collective expectations known to all members, the risk of unwanted outcomes and blaming can be significantly reduced and as such, help maintain or improve team relations.

- Leadership — Modeling Desired Team Behaviors: Teams need a leader who can and will show them the way. When it comes to such, actions speak louder than words. To help build your team into one cohesively effective unit, you'll need to walk the talk and show them the way with your behaviors and actions. If your subordinates see how positively you respond to blindsiding curveballs, they can't help but be the same but when they see you react very negatively with much pessimism, don't expect to have a bunch of optimistic and resilient team members.

- Structural Changes, e.g., Reporting Relationships, Required Relationships, Required Interactions, Pairing, Task Enrichment: As you let every member of the team know what is expected of them individually and collectively, it's important to provide a structure that can help them perform and behave according to such expectations. If you want to fly an airplane, you need to have an airport and in the same manner, creating an optimal organizational or team structure will go a long way in helping each member behave and perform as expected individually and as a team.

- Empowering Group As A Whole By Allowing Occassional Group Decision Making and Problem Solving: True, group thinking as a general practice is risky but it doesn't mean it doesn't have any practical value. Used every now and then, it can help facilitate a stronger tie among team members by letting them work together towards making decisions for the team and solving problems.

- Changes To The Performance Management System Especially In The Area Of Reward/Behavior Links: Make no mistake about it, people need to be motivated and using the right incentives, you can spur your teams' members to perform excellently and consistently. Use the wrong incentives, however, and you run the risk of stagnation or worse, deteriorating team performance. As you know the members of your team even more, you'll have a better sense of what it is that will really motivate them to do their best for the team.

- Formal Training in Deficient Areas: A team, just like any chain, is only as strong as its weakest link. By training team members in areas that the team is lacking in, you make the team perform better, which can lead to stronger ties among members and lead to further improvements in performance.

- Team Member Coaching by Team Leader or Peers: Nothing beats mentoring subordinates to help build their skills and confidence further. Coaching involves both theoretical and practical application, 2 sides of the learning coin. As such, learning becomes faster and more effective. As the subordinate's performance improves, they appreciate their mentors more and vice versa, leading to a stronger team bond and better team performance.

- Behavior Modification through Shaping: Shaping is a technique where behavior change is broken down into many smaller increments. The rationale behind it is that if you wait for a person to exhibit a certain behavior that may be too great a step given his current behavior before rewarding him or her, the desired change may not happen. Shaping involves breaking down the desired behavioral change into smaller parts of increasing difficulty, rewarding the person progressively. With smaller steps, you increase the chances of your members' behavior changing by shaping it gradually instead of in one big lump.

- Constructive Feedback: Let's face it, you'll need to give feedback to team members that may not be taken positively such as slow project turnovers or frequent tardiness. One way to do this effectively is to use the hamburger principle, wherein the main corrective feedback is the hamburger patty sandwiched by two halves of a hamburger bun, which represent positive feedback or complements. For example, instead of saying "You're frequently late, John.", you can say "I appreciate your dedication to your job and your family John (first half of the bun). I believe you can do much better and live up to your potential by coming to work on time more often (the burger patty). Thanks for being a responsible and committed member of the team, John, and I'm looking forward to seeing you at the office on time more frequently (second half of the burger bun)."

- Changing Membership (Transfers, Infusion of New Members, etc.): There'll be situations where in certain members aren't just cut out for the team in terms of performing specific tasks and may require the acquisition of new and more capable members. Doing so is the fastest way of strengthening and building up your team.

- Holiday Giveaway – As And When Required: Your team members are people and not machines. Give them, nay, force them if you must, to take holidays off once every year to relax and recharge. They'll appreciate you for it and chances are, come back even more inspired to work.

Here again, managers are unlikely to have the time, energy, or resources to apply all improvement strategies simultaneously. As a manager, you don't have to worry about applying them all. In many cases, one or two of the above-mentioned strategies is enough to significantly build up your team.

Another thing to consider about these strategies is that each improvement strategies won't be equally effective when applied to any one teams characteristics. Managers should therefore once more articulate and apply a number of decision criteria that would help them decide on the appropriate mix of improvement interventions. Knowing team members individually and collectively as well as the team's operating environment is key to successfully utilizing these strategies as appropriate.

The above-mentioned points provide criteria that managers might find helpful when attempting to compare and select intervention strategies. The criteria are quite similar to those discussed in the earlier chapters, but put greater emphasis on costs and benefits, organizational fit, and alignment with managerial and group member competencies, risk propensity, and preparedness.

The intervention strategies selected will reflect the unique characteristics of the situation being considered and the managerial philosophies of key decision makers. As was the case above, it is essential for managers to have their "Ks" in place.

Selecting appropriate intervention strategies

The intervention strategies are based on the following criteria

- Likelihood of Success: Managers should obviously choose strategies that they feel will succeed. Otherwise, what's the point, right?

- Cost Benefit or Utility Analysis: Apart from likelihood of success, managers also need to know if just how beneficial implementing such strategies can be. If strategy A has a 95% chance of likelihood with an expected benefit of $100,000 and strategy B has a 90% likelihood chance but an expected benefit of $150,000, guess which strategy must the manager choose?

- Time Requirements for Completion: A strategy with no deadline is one that's doomed to fail. Without deadlines, there'll be no sense of urgency when it comes to implementation. And when it comes to deadlines, it would benefit managers to keep in mind Parkinson's Law, which states that a tasks perceived importance increases as less time is given to complete it. In other words, shorter deadlines can lead to better performance. Though procrastination is definitely discouraged, this is the reason why many people seem to perform better when they procrastinate. The increased sense of urgency that comes with a looming deadline forces the brain to focus on what's essential, which leads to seemingly better performance.

- Leader Preferences or Competencies: It will be hard for managers or leaders to implement intervention strategies for which they aren't competent to handle. Their ability to implement certain strategies should also be an important consideration. If the appropriate strategy falls outside of a manager's competency or preference, tapping an external facilitator who's competent in the chosen strategy should be considered.

- Organizational Culture and History: The general psyche of the organization to which the team belongs can play a big role in an intervention strategy's success or failure. If the general culture is oblivious or even averse to what seems to be the most appropriate intervention strategy, the members may not accept the strategy and refuse to cooperate or if ever they do, they'll do so only half-heartedly and may even be with resentment.

- Availability of Internal/External Hard Resources to Support Intervention Strategy (Money, Trainers, Facilities, Equipment, etc.): Managers should make sure that the necessary resources are available to implement the chosen strategy successfully. Otherwise, it will be an exercise in futility and a waste of time and organizational resources.

- Team Member Characteristics and Preparedness: If the team members concerned aren't cut out and prepared for a particular intervention strategy, it won't work. Remember, intervention requires the involvement of everyone concerned and if one party isn't cut out for a chosen strategy, chances are that they won't be able to successfully fulfill their end of the bargain and will lead to a failed strategy that may even worsen the conflict it sought to resolve in the first place.

- Likelihood of Group Member Support: As mentioned previously, everyone has to be on board when a particular intervention strategy is chosen. If not, it's doomed to fail. Managers need to get the members' support if the chosen strategy is to work, assuming everything else is in place.

- Political Pressures and Organizational Realities: In a perfect world, organizational politics shouldn't even be a factor when it comes to effective intervention. Unfortunately, all members of an organization are only human and are subject to biases, preferences and politics. To the extent that a manager is aware of the organization's political environment is the extent he or she will be able to assess beforehand if a particular intervention strategy will be effective or not.

- Impression Management Issues: Lastly, intervention strategies – no matter how likely to be successful, well funded and complementary to organizational political culture – can be significantly affected by how the facilitator or the manager is perceived by both parties. If the facilitator or manager is perceived by both parties to be trustworthy, objective and fair, then the strategy has high chances of being successful. On the other hand, an opposite perception can render it ineffective from the get go.

Implementing strategies

Implementation is a critical component of any team-building intervention. This is where the rubber meets the road and is the point at which analysis and planning become reality. If the proof of the pudding is in the eating, implementation – successful ones at that – is a particular intervention strategies' validation of success.

Each intervention will have its own unique sequence of steps designed to bring it on line and obtain the desired improvement in the selected team characteristic. A brief example is provided as an insight into the implementation process:

Preparation

Chances of success are higher with the right set up and to begin the intervention process for more open communications, the manager must first be able to identify what he or she believes are the necessary supporting behaviors. This can be accomplished through a detailed job analysis, analysis of critical incidents, direct observation, personal introspection, or by seeking input from experts or other successful managers. Output from such activities should provide the manager with the required support behaviors necessary to help improve goal consensus.

Communicate Behaviors

Once identified, it is critical that the manager's behavioral expectations are clearly communicated to group members. If not, members are at risk of behaving differently from what's required out of ignorance and this could derail the successful implementation of the intervention strategy.

Successfully communicating expected behaviors can be accomplished through a formal goal setting meeting, brief informal exchanges with group members, or direct feedback to deficient individuals. The important thing regardless of the chosen method is that expectations are clearly understood.

When communicating one's behavioral expectations it is also necessary to indicate why the behaviors are important, the consequences of desired behaviors, the conditions under which they should be exhibited, and how group members will be assessed. The key is to make the employee understand, accept, and be willing to engage in the new behaviors. When this happens, the employee is able to appreciate the expected new behavior from him or her, which increases the likelihood of successfully exhibiting the new expected behavior.

Measurement/Feedback

The manager should link the next two steps. He or she observes, records, and rates group members' behavior. When sufficient information has been collected to draw meaningful conclusions, the manager then provides meaningful feedback to group members. During this feedback encounter the manager should indicate his or her willingness to help group members improve their performance through one-on-one coaching.

The manager should faithfully get information or feedback as to the group members' behaviors because these would serve as some sort of a GPS in that it gives him or her an accurate enough idea of where the team and its members are in light of implementing a chosen strategy. If not, then progress may be affected because either the manager will make the mistake of overestimating the success or underestimate the shortcomings of implementing the strategy.

Coaching Encounter

Any coaching exchange initiated by group members, or the team leader, should be voluntary and reflect the assumption that the coach and employee are joint partners in the process. When this process is made compulsory, the element of trust and respect may be significantly reduced or even removed, which can significantly undermine the implemented strategy's effectiveness.

The two parties will jointly

a) Assess current behavior;

b) Try to understand why desired behavior or activities did not occur, and determine if any environmental barriers exist; and

c) Establish new behavioral expectations for each other. It is at this point that the group member states his or her willingness to change personal behavior.

Monitor and Recycle

No intervention strategy is worth initiating unless managers are willing to monitor its success. Therefore managers working through this process must again observe, record, and evaluate group member behaviors. This information will help managers identify new required behaviors, fine-tune the coaching process, or directly act as the basis for group member feedback.

Ross Elkins

Chapter 5

Crises and How to Manage a Crisis Efficiently

Crisis management is one of the toughest jobs a manager will have to perform. This is because crises don't' follow rules and regulations. They happen due to different circumstances and under different conditions that a manager can't claim expertise in handling the next one because it will be totally different from the other. As such, crises managers need to be very confident and quick on their feet when it comes to managing crises efficiently.

Throughout your training, you will have gone through the mundane routine so that it is what your brain will be accustomed to. It takes a certain type of test of leadership skill in order to perform well in a crisis.

Hence, it is very crucial that in order to prove yourself, you know exactly how to handle any crisis that may arise in your path to becoming an effective and efficient manager.

Here is a list of characteristics you need to remember that will help you deal with any and all sorts of crises:

- **Be Critical and Realistic:** As a manager, you are the leader and a leader is never found at the back of the crowd. He is at the front line, leading his team forward. Hence, you should always deal with a crisis head-on. This will inspire the members of your team to keep calm and perform well under crises too.

  This is possible only if you clear any and all illusions you have about the crisis. Gather as much facts and information about the crises being experienced because only through these will you be able to sift the illusions from reality, the myths from certainties.

  As you gather such facts and information and sift away the illusions about the crisis, critically analyze all the points of your crisis and plan your strategy according to that. Otherwise, you'll fail to contain the crisis and may let it escalate even further. Don't just go all gung-ho with no solid plan of action, simply hoping for the results to work out. Create a foolproof plan based on the information and facts you gathered so that you won't have to rely on luck for your success.

- **Strategy and Detail:** As a manager, your strategy matters most. You need to see the problem and then look at it from a bigger picture – see the forest and not the trees as Stephen Covey once wrote. A good and effective manager knows both what is at the top of the mountain and at the base of it. Hence, your vision should be all encompassing.

  You also need to look at the wave and see the ripples it will cause – know the cause and all possible repercussions of your alternative courses of action as much as possible. True, you can't perfectly predict all the possible results of a course of action but that shouldn't stop you from exhausting all possible ideas. If you don't, you run the risk of pouring gasoline over the crisis flame and escalate it even further.

Even if you haven't ever faced a crisis of this sort before, you should accept the fact that regardless of your inexperience of such a crisis, you're the one who will need to solve it and thus you should take courage and the lead in managing it. The buck stops with you as the manager and you can't resort to blaming when things go down.

This will mean getting down into the fray and learning all there is to learn about it. Get information about your crisis and think about how you can untangle this knot of problems. Remember that your problem will only get solved with minimal damage if you know what cause and effect is. Hence, make a plan of what you are to do and what result that will cause. Thus, your crisis will seem small and you will be able to handle anything easily.

- **Weigh Your Options:** As a manager, you know by now that there are two sides to everything but when it comes to crises, there are more than 2 sides to consider. Know that there will be many ways to handle a crisis but you need to handle it gracefully so that you handle it quickly, efficiently and without damage to your own goals. Choosing how you handle it without careful thought is the single biggest obstacle to your being able to contain it fast and well.

This might mean that you will have to consult with your own team and others as well. Never be afraid to ask for advice, there's no shame in doing so. The real shame is when you screw up and escalate the crisis even more because you were too proud to ask for help. Ask even if this means that you have to go and talk to other managers like yourself, educate yourself on a crisis and ask for advice.

Though at the end you might want to follow your initial plan and do what you wanted to in the beginning, you will have a very clearer view of what you are doing and change plans accordingly if needed. As you do, you'll avoid worrying about whether or not you could've handled it better. This is extremely crucial for your own peace of mind since a crisis will stress you out in a great way so you need to eliminate all doubts from your system. Confidence in your ability to take control and peace of mind is key here.

- **Make Decisions:** Take this as an extension of the last point but you will have to make decisions and make them at the right time. There is nothing worse in a crisis than a wrongly timed decision because a right decision made a second too late is still a wrong one.

  To make a decision, you will have to listen to your gut and take the decision that you honestly know and believe to be the best alternative. This only comes after years upon years of experience. A new manager cannot take the best decision because they will always be indecisive due to his or her relative inexperience in handling crises. Hence, here is the time when you need to call upon all your years of training and find any instances where you dealt with or saw someone dealing with some crisis of the similar sort if you are new to managing crises or at being a manager in general.

Decision making, however, is not simply setting things in motion. You also need to sell the decision to other people that are critical to successfully handling a crisis such as your superiors and to some extent, your subordinates who'll be carrying out your decision. If you don't, you run the risk of failing to get their full support, which may prove to be the undoing of your crisis management plan of action.

Make a decision, detail WHY you took that particular decision and also enlist the results this decision will cause. Try to pick a decision that will cause the least amount of damage possible. Then, go in with full confidence in your choice. Remember that in the end, it all comes down to rational and realistic thinking and hence any decision based on this is the decision that is best. The clearer you're able to present your case and the more confident you are in them, the greater are your chances of winning their support.

- **Collaborate:** Like we mentioned before, never be afraid to ask advice of anyone. If making the best decision means asking help from team-member or another manager, do it. Remember, humility is as important a character trait of an effective manager as is confidence. In fact, it takes a lot of confidence to be humble enough and ask for other people's help.

Be very clear of your goals, which are to reach a particular point. And if you think that someone can help you reach your goal in good time and in a better way, ask for help. You won't regret doing so, especially if it leads to your being able to successfully resolve or manage a crisis.

Collaboration can mean both working with your team, a particular team-member that you feel can help you in this specific time of need or another manager who might have more experience or experience in a similar way. It doesn't matter if the person or people you collaborate with are from your team or outside of it. What matters is you collaborate with people who'll be able to help successfully handle crises.

Work on the principle that two heads are better than one and if nothing else, you will have another set of eyes to view the problem from. You have blind spots, as with everyone else and having another set of eyes can help you see these blind spots and enable you to manage crises much better. This means that perhaps your decision might be improved or you might find a much easier solution to your problem, both of which will be in your favor.

Collaboration will also help you to beat stress since a second opinion can help you see that your problem might not be as big as you imagined and this will help you reach a conclusion in a better way. Many times, we feel overwhelmed with certain situations because we are either too close to the problem or inside it. The opinion of someone who's detached from the situation can help assure you that the crisis you're handling may not be as big as you thought it is.

- **Take Note Of Adverse Opinion:** Remember how we talked about the value of conflicts or differing opinions and preferences within a team? A bad and inefficient manager is one who only surrounds him or herself with those who agree with them because these people either have the same blind spots as him or herself or people with no convictions. Such people are easily pressured into making wrong decisions or acting unwisely and are thus practically worthless to the manager.

If you love surrounding yourself with people who always or most of the time agree with you, beware. This might make you feel good in the short term but in the long run, you will find yourself in a very lonely position indeed. This means that since you will only find people who agree with everything you say, you will always have to make decisions yourself and you will only have your own opinion reflected back at you. You're not able to enjoy the benefit of being able to really see things as they are and act or decide accordingly. You're at high risk of bungling crises or fail to even manage your team well even if there're no crises.

Avoid this. Heed the advice to "keep your enemies closer". Keep your critics close because they will show you where you are wrong and this will help you improve greatly. You will never be one hundred percent effective but you always need to strive for that extra ten percent. This means listening to everyone who criticizes you.

Keep in mind that not every critic will be accurate, however. Some people will try to bring you down most deliberately. These are not your friends, either. This is where a good confidence in your own abilities and judgments will come into play. When you're aware of your own capabilities as well as limits, you'll be in a great position to determine the true value of your critics' opinions about you and your courses of action.

As such, take every advice and analyze it critically so you neither miss something important nor grow insecure because of the gossip or language of others. The goal is to get accurate feedback that will help you become an even more effective manager or leader.

- **Stay Calm and Positive:** Being critical is the first step and it is a most important one. However, never let yourself grow pessimistic because even if they seem similar, being critical and pessimist are two different things. Being critical is simply trying to identify all things that can possibly go wrong with the intention of being able to address them should they happen while being pessimist is simply believing more in the negative side of things without the intention of eventually addressing them.

Whilst in a crisis, you are the leader and your team will be looking up to you. If you get too critical, there is a great chance you will grow increasingly pessimistic. This will cause you to grow depressed which will sap your energy. But not only this, such a habit will affect your team as well.

That's why a much as critical thinking is important when handling crises, you shouldn't go overboard. Be very sensitive to your team members' reactions to see if you're overdoing it because your team will be, especially in the case of a crisis, monitoring and copying your every move. If you go into the ordeal head-on, they will be courageous too. If you remain calm, they will feel like everything is under control. However, the slightest sign of trouble and their morale will start to wane and decrease as well. Hence you'll need to also rein in your critical thinking to prevent pessimism.

Stay calm – or at least pretend to be so – and you will eventually clear your own head and will be able to look at the crisis in a much better way than you had been before. Hence, even when it feels like the walls are caving in, keep a level head and find your nearest and safest exit and you will make it. Just continue holding the fort while in the midst of crises.

- **Take Risks:** Timely decisions are wonderful but the reality is it involves risk, which is defined as the chance of something unfavorable happening. You can't eliminate risk – you can only manage it either by doing things that will lower the chances of it materializing or preparing to manage its potential effects should materialize. A crisis is a crisis only because you have not dealt with it previously. Thus, it's alright to be afraid but be continue to be rational about your fear, which is only based on the fact that you have not been there before. Eventually, your mind will reassure itself about your ability to handle a crises because even though you haven't experienced the same kind before, you have been in other crises that you've managed well.

Hence, take risks and deliver yourself from this problem. Test waters before you jump in but when the results arrive, make haste in jumping in so that you may reach the results you desire.

As the economic rule goes, greater the risk, greater the profit. As such, you will need to plan out just exactly what it is that you are attempting to do if you want a bigger payoff. But when you do take that decision, give it your hundred percent because anything less significantly increases the possibility of associated risks materializing.

- **Choose The Safest Option:** This might seem easier said than done but in fact, it is one of the best ways of dealing with a crisis. To do this, you will need to clear your mind of any and all sorts of apprehensions.

  How can you do this? By taking a break, turning off your cell phone and just writing down whatever options you have. Get away from any and all distractions so you can create a mini feasibility report and see which option causes the least damage whilst giving the best result in the most objective way you can. Distractions, especially those related to the crises you're handling, have a way of making people decide with much bias. The objective you identify and evaluate your options, the higher your risk of failing to manage crises well. It's because some options might seem to give a hundred percent result but the damage would be great too and a clouded or biased judgment is usually unable to see those possible damages.

  Avoid this. Remember that you need to play it safe. Pick the option with the lowest risk such as a result that might give an 80% of the result but only 5% damage as compared to 95% chances of success but with a possible damage of 20%. Ratios can be very handy when making such decisions because these are based on numbers (read:

objective) and give you a clearer picture of what you are gaining and what you are losing.

However, when you do end up making a decision, stick to it and implement each and every aspect of it without doubting yourself. Remember that the time to hesitate has long since passed and therefore what you have is only what you have and you should utilize it to a hundred percent.

- **Admit Mistakes:** Remember that you are human. You will make mistakes. Don't demonize these and fear them to death. You can choose to look at mistakes as learning opportunities. I don't know with you but I believe mistakes are better teachers than the things we do right. With every crisis that you face, you will learn and get better. Hence, don't try to hide your mistakes; even if you make one, it is a crucial part of learning. Embrace them but don't long for and go after them. Do your best to avoid them and if you can't, simply take in the valuable lessons associated with them by asking empowering questions such as "How can I do things better to avoid making the same mistake in the future?" Hence, as soon as you realize your fault, correct it and move on to the next step of crisis management.

At the end, remember that no matter what happens, you will never possess all ten of these characteristics right away. There will be a few points that will elude you for a long time until managing a crisis becomes as natural as making a cup of coffee. Also, with every crisis, you will learn more about handling the crises that are to come. Remember, practice doesn't necessarily make perfect but it can lead to mastery and excellence. The more you accept the fact that you can make mistakes along the way, the more you'll be able to make more effective decisions and learn from inevitable mistakes much better.

There's a lot of debate as to whether leaders are made or born. A lot of leaders possess these characteristics naturally and that is what makes them leaders. But there are a lot of people who never exhibited such traits in their childhood and even early adult years but because of circumstances or purposeful learning, they eventually learned how to become great leaders. Hence, if you aren't afraid to take risks and are willing to deal with anything head-on, you will be a master of these characteristics and more in record time even if you think you're not a naturally gifted leader. Hence, the one characteristic you need to possess in the largest quantity is that of courage because a great and efficient manager is one who is not afraid to take risks and lead his team through even the choppiest waters to get things done.

Chapter 6

Delegation: How Much Control to Relinquish

Delegation is a skill that is an immensely bitter pill to swallow for a lot of people especially managers who are control freaks. There are a lot of emotional and political barriers that make a manager want to avoid a delegation. A lot of this is based around the fact that even after the job has been completed you will be responsible and accountable for the outcome. As such, you want to make sure things are done right, which is enough reason for you to avoid delegating tasks to the members or your team.

However, management experts around the globe agree that once you get the hang of the thing, delegation can be one of the most useful tools which will help you achieve your goals and do so in a quicker and more efficient way. In fact, as far back as the biblical times, delegation has been practiced as a way to get things done efficiently. Consider this passage from Exodus 18:17-22 in the Bible where Jethro, Moses' father-in-law, advised Moses on how to best handle the people after seeing him being too burdened with the petty stuff of having to settle disputes among the numerous people of Israel that kept him from doing what he's really supposed to do:

> Moses' father-in-law said to him, "What you are doing is not good. You and the people with you will certainly wear yourselves out, for the thing is too heavy for you. You are not able to do it alone. Now obey my voice; I will give you advice, and God be with you! *You shall represent the people before God and bring their cases to God, and you shall warn them about the statutes and the laws, and make them know the way in which they must walk and what they must do* (Moses' real calling, emphasis mine). Moreover, *look for able men from all the people, men who fear God, who are trustworthy and hate a bribe, and place such men over the people as chiefs of thousands, of hundreds, of fifties, and of tens. And let them judge the people at all times. Every great matter they shall bring to you, but any small matter they shall decide themselves* (delegating tasks, emphasis mine). So it will be easier for you, and they will bear the burden with you.

You don't have to be a Christian to see that delegating tasks is a wise practice that's been around for ages and the fact that it's still being practiced now is a testament to its efficacy.

That being said, it is always confusing for a manager to start delegating until they get the proper hang of the thing. There is, in fact, a whole list of dos and don'ts that apply when you start to delegate tasks to other people. Here is an outline that will help you which tasks you should delegate to other people and which ones you shouldn't even think about delegating:

Which Tasks Can You Delegate?

The first step of delegating is acknowledging the fact that as a manger, you'll need to do the really important (often times, hardest) stuff yourself. Delegation means to relinquish control so that, like Moses, you can focus on fulfilling your higher organizational calling. Hence, the tasks you should delegate should be ones that would be easily handled by even the most inexperienced of employees.

While delegating, remember that the tasks or responsibilities you'll delegate to your subordinates should be simple, quantifiable and easily performed in the time limit that you set. Make sure to explain clearly and thoroughly what needs to be done even if it means explaining yourself over and over and risk sounding redundant. Remember that delegation is a tool that is for your advantage and not to stress you out further and by being redundant in the beginning, you'll be able to reduce the risk of costly mistakes that need to be fixed later on. If you start worrying over delegation as well, that will be the opposite of what delegation is meant to do in the first place because it should give you peace of mind to be able to attend to higher order stuff.

Here is a list to give you some idea of the tasks you can delegate:

Recurring Decisions and Actions:

There are some tasks that are easy but you still have to do them on a frequent basis. It is always a good idea to hand these easy tasks over to your subordinates because however simple or easy they may seem, they can be quite voluminous and take up a lot of your valuable time – time that you can otherwise devote to higher level responsibilities. Delegating tasks like these takes a significant burden off of your shoulders and also trains your subordinates. Hence, this is a win-win situation for everyone.

Priorities That Take Too Much Time:

Speaking of time, if you were to go to that list of priorities, you might find that there are some priorities that though important are easy enough for other people to handle. These are the priorities you should hand off as a delegation. Remember that just because it is a priority, doesn't mean it's hard and if it's easy, someone else might be able to do it so you get twice the amount of priorities handled with your combined effort in half the amount of time than it would take if you did it yourself. By delegating such tasks, you are effectively able to double, even triple your productivity.

Special Tasks:

There is a list of one-time tasks that you will have to perform only once in a while. If these are easy enough that anyone else can handle them, let them handle them for you and save time. Remember, the key is to focus on what's truly most important for the team and if you regularly take on tasks like these, you'll be burdened just like Moses.

Long-Distance Tasks:

A good manager is always in demand. They will need to be in many places at once but since teleportation has not yet been perfected, that is impossible. Hence, in order to save time to travel, you can employ a delegation that visits far-off places for you and handles some matters so you don't have the additional burden of travel to deal with. Effectively, you're able to bi-locate (be at two or more places at the same time) just like the famous Catholic saint Padre Pio. Only your bi-location powers aren't enough to get you canonized as a saint and is limited to personal productivity only.

Details:

It is a sad fact that details, do not, in fact, take care of themselves. Equally unfortunate is that taking care of details, especially the minute ones, can be time consuming. As such, it's best to delegate taking care of details that aren't so important but are time consuming to your team members. If you need to take care of details as a manager, stick to those that really matter and chances are, there aren't a lot of them to burden your personal productivity as a manager.

There are a lot of minute details that you will need to take care of while you are managing a project yourself. So, if you have the choice of having a delegation, you can always ask them to keep an eye on the less important details so that you can focus on the more important ones with a clear mind.

Delegate to Train:

You are a manager and a superb one but you aren't perfect and in fact, you'll realize that there are certain areas of your team's functions that you need help in. If you notice that one particular team member has a particular penchant or talent for a specific skill pertaining to such areas that you need help in, assign related tasks to them. You may start small but you may notice that with time, you will want to increase the difficulty of the tasks as you see that the person you delegated it to becomes better and better at it. This will mean not only that you will have a valuable asset in your arsenal but also that your team member will be grateful to you for the training. It's clearly a win-win situation for you, the team member and the team as a whole.

Above were the tasks that you can easily delegate to anyone. However, there are some tasks that you cannot and should not assign to other people. Here are the limitations to delegation:

Tasks that are Personal:

This doesn't mean sending someone off to pick up your laundry because you shouldn't be doing that anyway. This means tasks that need your specific touch. As a manager, a task is assigned to you because of the way you handle it. Your team is just your tool. Hence, any tasks that require your views, your attention and your style, you shouldn't hand over to your delegation.

Some of these tasks include reporting to upper management about how the team is performing and challenges, if any, that keep the team from performing optimally. Also included in these tasks are presenting important proposals that can help the team perform better to upper management and making crucial decisions for which you alone are accountable.

Risky Tasks:

Some priority tasks are only so because there is a certain risk involved in performing them; a risk that is only eliminated because of YOUR expertise. Because novice members of your team or those that don't have as much experience as you do, they may not be able to handle high risk and priority tasks as good as you do. Even if they do manage to fulfill the tasks, they might end up messing them up and at the end of the day, you will be accountable for the team's performance to upper management. Hence, it is better to take these tasks yourself just to remain on the safe side and ensure your team's continued success.

Have Legal Restrictions:

There are some tasks that only you are ALLOWED to do. This means that you are restricted by law to pass them off to someone else. Hence, this is a big no-no. Never assign the tasks that you are legally bound to do, to someone else no matter how talented they might be. Examples of these may include disbursement of the organization's funds up to a certain amount or delegating your authority to disburse funds to a member of the accounting team.

Tasks that are Specifically Assigned to You:

There might be some tasks that might be assigned to you and you alone even if though you might feel that someone else can handle them. These include a lot of tasks your bosses might want you to do efficiently such as overseeing the construction and opening of a new company branch or presenting a quarterly report to the Board Of Directors. Remember that if someone has trusted you with a task, it is your responsibility to complete it. Delegating such particular tasks to a member of your team, regardless of that person's capabilities, won't just compromise your team's performance – it'll also compromise your good standing with your superiors.

A delegation is a wonderful tool to have at your disposal because it helps you leverage yourself and increase your personal and team productivity by fulfilling tasks at high speed without stressing you out. This also means that you can perform your work efficiently. It's like you're able to effectively multiply your working self!

Delegation however, is not – and should never be – an excuse to slack off on the work that you are meant to do yourself. Practically, whenever you hand off something you are meant to do to someone else, even if the tasks are only slightly varied than what you had in mind, the end result might be a full 180 degrees from what you expected.

Delegation is like a very sharp kitchen knife, i.e. it can be used either for good (culinary delight) or evil (harming others and yourself). As such, delegate wisely using the guidelines presented in this chapter.

Chapter 7

Harassment and Altercations

Harassment is an alarmingly common problem in an office setting and one that has the potential to not just slow your team down but to wreak havoc in it and members of your team. As a manager, it is your job that all your employees feel safe and secure. You should be their first go-to in case they face any problems regarding this issue. For that to happen, you need to be perceived as a manager who's fair, trustworthy and just. Such perceptions require a good working and personal relationship with your team members.

Here are the two most common types of harassment you will have to deal with and tips on how to deal with them:

- **Sexual Harassment:**

  One of the most common types of harassment, which you as a manager will have to deal with, is sexual harassment. It's not unheard of, it's not uncommon and yet, a lot of managers, when faced with this issue are at a complete loss as to what to do about it. One of the reasons is experience. Although it's one of the most common forms of harassment around, it's quite uncommon to hear of managers whose teams report sexual harassment cases more than once. As such, most managers are unprepared and ill equipped to handle reported cases of such harassments.

Given that most managers have no actual experience by the time their team reports a case of sexual harassment, the other alternative to help them deal with such cases well is training. Unfortunately, many managers don't have the luxury of being trained to handle such incidents. If you're one of those managers, it's best that you get training on the matter in whatever ways that may be practically possible for you – journals, articles, books, seminars or courses on the subject. Additionally, if you can't seem to find anything, even the steps mentioned in this article will help you to tackle any types of cases of sexual harassment that you will come across, effectively.

How to deal with sexual harassment:

- Even before any sort of complaint is filed, be sure that you have made your company's policy on sexual harassment clear. It's been said that an ounce of prevention is better than a ton of cure. Doing your best as manager to educate your team members on your organization's sexual harassment policies and guidelines can go a long way towards reducing the risk for such an event happening in your team. It will also help you a great deal to include a list specific acts that may be considered as sexual harassment.

Paste notices on the bulletin board, email memos, hold seminars on the thing and make it clear that any complaint that arises will not be tolerated but it will be investigated until either all charges are cleared or proven. Make it crystal clear that your company is strictly intolerant of anything that makes your employees uncomfortable.

- If and when a sexual harassment case does arise, form an internal committee consisting of a few trusted members of your staff and assign the case to this committee. All staff members should be people who are aware of the company and company's history and should have a clean reputation themselves. Make sure to head the committee yourself, actively participating in the hearings as much as possible to ensure you're on top of the situation and to assure both parties of a fair process.

- Make the complainant feel at ease and secure. Even in today's world, it takes a lot of courage to come out with reports of sexual harassment and misconduct because a person is always afraid that it would reflect on their record or there would be a retaliation launched against them. Compared to other forms of harassments, sexual cases are the most sensitive and have the potential to psychologically affect both the complainant and the accused, especially if the latter is innocent. Reputations can be smirched and damaged unnecessarily, which is why you need to make sure such cases are handled confidentially and in the most transparent and respectful way.

- Ask the complainant to inform you immediately if they face any sort of retaliation or further harassment either at the hand of the first accused or anyone else. Tell them that they were brave to come to you and that you will make sure that nothing of the sort ever happens again. More over, talk to the person who retaliated or harassed the complainant and take the proper actions to discourage any further threats to the complainant.

- Ask the employee to relay the whole story to you in his or her own words. Record the interview if need be or take notes but if you plan on taking notes, be thorough as the employee might not want to repeat their ordeal over and over again. Write down anything that feels important such as time, date, place, situation, any witnesses if they'd been around, etc. I can't overemphasize the need to capture each and every important detail of the employee's story as these will either prove the guilt of the accused or establish his or her innocence.

- Contact the person accused and tell them that no acts of retaliation or further harassment will be tolerated. Assure them that you will be transparent, thorough, honest, fair in hearing their side along with the complainant's and that everything will be kept in strict confidence. You'll also need to tell them that regardless of their innocence or guilt, retaliating against or harassing the complainant will only serve to increase the chances of them being convicted of the complaint.

- Interview the accused as you did the accuser. Don't, even for a moment, let them feel like you actually believe that they have been proved as a harasser because this will be viewed as biasedness. Ask if they have any alibis as to where they were when the alleged harassment took place.

- It's important that both the accused and the complainant perceive you as a fair and honest judge. As such, do everything that you can to assure them that you will conduct the hearings in a fair, transparent, confidential and respectful manner. The moment you lose any of the parties' trust and confidence, the integrity of your hearings will be compromised and you run the risk of this case being elevated to higher ups and tarnish the image and reputation of both you as a manager and your team as a whole.

- Be sure to get the testimonies of all witnesses that have been provided by either side by interviewing them thoroughly as well. Tell them not to let their personal views about either party cloud their judgment but nevertheless, be sure to take into consideration the fact that these witnesses will have their own biases in favor of the party which they are testifying for. Listen only to facts, note them down and ask open-ended questions about those facts and information in order to validate the veracity and overall consistency of the testimonies.

- Finally, discuss the results and your findings with other people of your committee. Additionally, consult with any other HR officials and reach a conclusion. Never conclude the investigation by yourself as you may have missed other important nuances of the facts and information gathered from the testimonies of everyone involved. Discussing the results and consulting with the committee members and other organization officials can help you see potential blind spots that may make or break the investigation. Just keep in mind as you confer with others that even 2 heads are better than one, too many chefs can spoil the broth too so limit your consultations to your committee members and one or two higher ranking officials within your organization to maintain confidentiality and integrity of the investigation.

- Decide whether the sexual harassment occurred or not and take appropriate actions. Remember that sometimes the more serious claims have to be forwarded to the authorities as per the request of the victim, no matter who they might be. Use your better judgment as whether or not you'll need to forward the incident to higher ups.

- Sometimes, some issues can be resolved by mediating. However, if the victim feels unsafe and the charges are extremely severe, you might have to terminate the harasser's contract as well. Tread carefully though because if you unjustly terminate the accused, you may be sued.

- Make sure that this never happens again through follow-up questions and proper documentation of the case. Take note of all the circumstances and events surrounding the incident, learn from them and make the necessary adjustments to minimize the risk of such an incident happening again. The more details and observations you note, the higher your chances of making sure that such incidents don't happen again. Not on your watch at least.

- Try to restore office environment as soon as the whole case is decided. Do not let your employees dwell over the negativity of the situation and take the lead in moving on past it. The previous ordeal will have been extremely worrisome and stressful for them too. Make sure that no other employee feels under the weather due to the office air. Welcome anyone to come forward and discuss their apprehensions either in front of everyone or in private if they feel more comfortable that way. Remember, the longer you remain in the situation, the harder it is to go back to normal team performance and may even cause a deterioration in performance over the long term.

- Take stricter measures once the case is over. Make a case study on sexual harassment and provide your team or department with a presentation on the results of your study as well as recommended courses of action to ensure this doesn't happen again or minimize its risk. Encourage other managers to do the same. Make posters, PowerPoint slides or even get printed pamphlets from various Non Profit Organizations that deal with sexual harassment. Educate your employees on what it means to cross their limits. Additionally, try and educate them on what actually counts as sexual harassment to reduce the risks of unnecessary incidents of sexual harassment that aren't even intentional. Prevention is key and knowledge helps prevention.

- Lastly, ask your team members and the parties involved for any advice if they feel that the case could have been handled in a better way. Remember, your observations and ideas are just one of several sides to the story and as such, you'll be able to have more – and possibly even better – ideas for prevention and better resolution of future cases, if any.

Listen to what they'll have to say and ponder over them to see if they have a valid point because let's face it – not everything you'll hear will be accurate or wise. Use better judgment concerning what advice and opinions to retain and which to discard. Give everyone a chance to air their opinion but carefully evaluate which to take seriously.

Also make it clear that just like this time, in case of any further occurrences, justice will be swift and on the spot. Tell them that anyone who feels uncomfortable for whatever reason can come forward at any time in any situation and that their concerns will be swiftly looked into. Also, assure employees that if they feel harassed but would like to remain anonymous, the company will respect their decision and will launch a more secretive investigation for them. Assure your employees that the company's first priority is their safety. This will go a long way in encouraging sexual harassment victims to come forward.

Racial and Religious Discrimination:

This is the second-most common type of discrimination that, you, as a manager will have to worry about in the work place. This is an extremely serious issue and one that has caused many companies to be fined because they have failed to protect their employees against this discrimination. The very subjective and emotional nature of religion makes it quite a challenge for many managers, especially in multi-racial and multi-religious teams.

Racial and religious discrimination can cause a company's environment to turn sour with one group enjoying privileges and power whilst another lives in fear. This gives your employees a huge amount of stress to deal with which means that they will not be able to focus on their work in such a situation. Further, if some radical religions are involved, then you may have to deal with more trouble than you may expect.

Here is a step-by-step process on how to deal with racial and religious discrimination:

- As you did with sexual harassment, make it clear that your company will never tolerate any instance of racial and/or religious discrimination. Clarify that for the management, one employee is just as precious as the other and any instances of discrimination or harassment based on these topics will be investigated thoroughly and strict action will be taken against the discriminators.

- It will also be beneficial if you get a chance to inform your employees what constitutes as religious discrimination. As with sexual harassment, religious discrimination may be due to innocent lapses in judgment and ignorance and may not necessarily be due to malicious intent. By being aware of what constitutes such discrimination, your team's members will be more careful about their words and actions and thus minimize the risk of such discriminations. Being aware also removes any excuse for such unacceptable behavior.

- Train your team to work together regardless of their background. To the extent possible, provide a working environment that encourages your team to discuss their problems with each other and come out with anything that troubles them. Make sure that they know they were chosen not because of their race or religion but because they are talented individuals with a set of characteristics that make them the best at what they do. Affirm them for their talents and skills, not their religious affiliations.

- Provide a mechanism or a system for employees to be able to report racial and religious discrimination in the office when these happen. These charges sometimes prove even more serious than sexual harassment. Remember, many wars in the past – even today – were waged not because of sex but in the name of religion. In this regard, be sure to assure your employees that they will be kept safe and even their names will be kept anonymous if need be when they come forward to report such incidences.

- Keep a strict check on people who show up as bullies in complaints again and again.

- If you need to interview an accused employee, never do it alone. Do it in the presence of another witness such as the HR manager.

- Record the interview and take notes. In particular, ask the accused person's views on race and other religions, which should give you a better idea if discrimination really did happen. Then ask them where they were when the instance of harassment occurred. Ask if they have any alibi or any witnesses. If they have, check them out to determine if they really substantiate the accused person's claim to innocence.

- Similarly, interview the accuser and make notes on their report as well.

- If you find that the harassment did occur, launch an investigation against the employee and inform them that after the initial warning, this will go on their permanent record. Also inform them of the repercussions of repeat offenses.

How to prevent further discrimination:

Once you have dealt with any existing issues, you'll need to do everything you can to ensure that this doesn't happen again and again. For this purpose, you will need to educate your staff and teach them that this sort of discrimination will not be tolerated in the work place. Orient them on the finer details of the incident so they may learn from it. Generalizations are often times vague and don't help the employees learn from the incident enough to prevent or avoid its recurrence.

Tell your employees that they are all humans first and should deal with each other in the same manner. This instance of harassment might also mean that you might want to break and reform your teams with a few members of different ethnic and religious groups in each, i.e., diversification. Don't put a single diverse employee in every group as this might occur in more bullying. However, introduce at least two employees in each group. When you do, you help prevent potential racial discrimination.

As mentioned earlier, provide an environment that's conducive to developing a good sense of teamwork and camaraderie. Set tasks that involve as many team members as possible so they get in the

Ross Elkins

habit of working together and in the process, become more intimate with each other. As they develop a closer relationship, they'll become more aware of the good side of each other's religion and beliefs. Most discrimination stems from ignorance and by getting to know each other on a deeper level, discrimination is practically prevented.

One of the best ways to address discrimination is to invite other people to give a talk on religious and racial discrimination. It's often the case that familiarity breeds contempt and because they're too familiar with you, they may not take what you have to say about discrimination as seriously as when an outsider does so.

Make posters and put them up around the office. Similarly place notices on the bulletin boards that emphasize investigations and proper sanctions await anyone caught disrupting office environment via discrimination.

Additionally, provide separate contact numbers and emails for anyone who feels that they are being discriminated against to give them a sense of security and confidence to report such incidences. Assure your employees that no matter who they are, their safety is your first concern and so they should come up with anything that is bothering them even if they choose to do so in private. Remember, religion is such a sensitive matter that it discourages most victims from coming forward to report their experiences. By providing a sense of security and confidentiality, you make it easier for and encourage them to come forward and help address such incidences.

Ask your employees to discuss their apprehensions freely so that the management has some idea on what their issues are.

Encourage them to discuss their problems; no matter how small so that it can be assured that no such events occur again.

Assure all your employees that their privacy will be respected but no discrimination will be tolerated against anyone.

Lastly, take measures to restore the office's professional environment as quickly as possible. Ask any employee, no matter who they are, to come up to you if they feel like they are uncomfortable with any aspect of the office. Tell them that if they are uncomfortable talking to you; they are free to talk to the HR manager or any other official they feel that can help them.

Again, the key is to encourage members of your team to come forward and report such unwanted incidents and give you and management the opportunity to address these as soon as possible.

Apart from your employees of a diverse race, your employees belonging to other religions might find that sometimes their religious obligations might clash with their office. Ask these employees to discuss their obligations with the HR manager so that they can allocate a few moments at work for their daily prayers, etc. The key to successfully maintaining an effective multi-racial or multi-religious team is to provide flexibility to accommodate such diversity within the context of the team's effectivity.

As a manager, you should be aware that in any country in the world, racial and religious discrimination is an offense that is often considered a punishable crime. As a leader, it is your utmost responsibility to ensure that all of your employees are feeling safe so that they can give their job a hundred percent. You aren't just their boss – you're also they defender and they'll look up to you for a certain level of security.

This might mean that you will have to get up close and personal with most, if not all, members of your team. Intentionally develop good relationships with them by discussing their religions, their cultures, anything that makes them unique so that you'll have a better understanding of who they are and make them feel that you are really there for them.

This is a great opportunity to learn and by doing so, you will also help other team members understand that just because their fellows are different, it doesn't mean that they are altogether unreachable. By reaching out to every member of your team and intentionally developing good relationships with them, you show them that multi-racial and multi-religious harmony is not impossible and provide an example to follow. Show the way because as the manager, you're the leader and the best way to lead is by example.

Chapter 8

How to Boost Employee Productivity

According to various researches, an employee spends more time with their co-workers and in their office than they do with their family at home. This means that because we spend so much time in an office environment, our work is likely to affect our moods and behavior.

Given that the nature of work is stressful, mostly, sometimes, as a manager, you might feel that your employees will start to lag and get tired easily. This will mean a slump in productivity as well. Such habits, though inevitable, are damaging to you and the company. Hence, here is a list of measures you can take to boost your employee's morale, make them more comfortable and so increase their productivity:

- **Improve The Environment:**

  Since they spend so much time in the office, your office will be your employee's second home. This means that you need to make their environment as comfortable and friendly as possible. While this does not mean that you treat your employee like a brother or provide beds for them to rest in, it does mean that you should help them get comfortable.

What does "comfortable" mean? It means encouraging your employees to 'personalize' their environments so even after putting in the longest hours they don't get homesick. This doesn't mean that they can put beds to sleep in and play loud, rocking sounds to stimulate their creative work juices. No no no...not that personalized. They should be able to do it subtly such as allowing them to put some of their favorite pictures on their work desks, to listen to their favorite music via earphones (at a low enough volume that they can still hear their phones ring or you calling them) and putting some seat contraptions that make for better sitting position. If you're organization has the budget, you can even provide for ergonomic furniture that can be adjusted according to your team members' physiques such as height adjustable seats and tables.

Remember, take care of the golden geese and they'll take care of you by continuing to churn out golden eggs. Disregard them and you run the risk of overworking or overstressing them until they burn out – and there goes the golden eggs.

Take measures that help your employees stay connected with you. You, as a manager, are also their leader. This means that it is your job to look after your employee so that they come up to you whenever they have a problem. Assure your employee, in subtle, non-verbal ways that you will have their back should they need to discuss a problem that is causing a hindrance in their progress. The more they feel personally connected to you, the more they'll be able to express themselves to you. Then you'll be able to get on top of almost everything that happens to your team that may affect it negatively.

- **Understand Your Employee and Where They Come From:**

Motivation is a key factor. Studies show that employees who have to support someone else are both more prone to work harder and more prone to give in to stress. This is natural. However, this can be prevented very easily by a manager's intervention. Some of your employees might even still be students, both working and studying and still supporting their homes.

How will you know when and how to intervene and help out your team member? I'll never get tired of this but it all boils down to intentionally developing relationships with them. Talk to your employees, ask about their experiences and then try and relay (in a way that doesn't seem demeaning and dismissive to their problems) your own experiences and views with the intention of encouraging them in their relatively challenging and stressful times. Often times, you don't even have to share your expert advice and life story. Simply telling your team member that you understand where they're coming from can, in many occasions, be enough to boost their morale and spirits. The simplest act of talking helps to unburden your employee so that they get refreshed and experience an energy boost so that they start working with renewed fervor and enthusiasm.

- **Back to the Drawing Board!**

Just like you, your employees have been trained to do their jobs. And guess what? Just like you, they too are human. It is a sad fact that though managers get to renew their trainings at seminars, employees don't usually enjoy the same benefits. Hence, they are liable to forget a few essential steps in their training. After all, either you use it or lose it. And when it comes to knowledge, what isn't applied tends to be forgotten.

This is where it becomes your job to sit your employees down and give them a refresher course on how they can deal with huge workloads or work that they don't like doing. Even if they have read tons of books on time and stress management, head knowledge won't simply cut it. Include as part of that refresher course an opportunity to actually practice the ideas you refresh them with. Let them experience how it is to practice them and enjoy their benefits.

Additionally, train your employees on how to deal with and divide stress. Give them points on how to divide work in small groups so that they do it quickly and efficiently without getting bored and losing productivity. Teach them techniques like the Pomodoro technique, where you work for 25 minutes straight and rest for 5, which constitutes 1 Pomodoro cycle. Working this way helps keep the mind fresh an energized and prevents it from getting fatigued quickly. You will find an immediate boost in your employee's productivity immediately after such a talk. This is because not only does your employee benefit from the talk but because they feel like their work is being valued and one of the biggest emotional needs of people is knowing that they matter. This gives your employees a new sense of responsibility and purpose, which means that they will work harder and smarter than before.

- **Small Incentives:**

There are only two motivations for a person's actions and habits – love of pleasure and fear of pain. Punishments for violating company rules, policies and guidelines appeal to the fear-of-pain part of motivation, which help minimize incidences of anarchy and chaos at the office. But what if you want to increase productivity? You can't threaten them to work better and more, right? So what are you to do? Appeal to the love-of-pleasure part of motivation through small incentives.

Talk to your higher officials about introducing small incentives. A lot of companies are doing this nowadays and have noticed how even a 20$ gift card for a spa or a restaurant is enough of an incentive to get employees to work harder. An employee whose looking forward to receiving something that appeals to them won't mind going the extra mile to increase personal productivity – they'll actually look forward to it.

This is effective because though an employee is already aware of their salary, they get an added bonus to work for. This helps give them a bit of a fresh breath of air and so they put in more of an effort. The saying "if you always do what you always did, you'll always get what you always got." can also be rephrased in this case into "if you always get what you always got, you'll probably continue to do what you always did." By giving them the chance to get something more than what they always got, chances are high that they'll do more than they normally would.

- **Initiate Discussions:**

  A tired employee is usually an undervalued one. An employee feels undervalued when they believe that their work is not being taken seriously. As such, it is your job as manager to be able to communicate to them that you do take their work seriously and that it matters.

  Discussing office work with your employees can help address this. Whether you do it on a personal level by discussing your own tasks or on a more strategic level where you discuss their tasks' strategy with your whole team, this will help your employee feel like they and their opinion are being valued enough to be consulted. My opinion, however, is that publicly affirming your team members can motivate them more than privately doing so. That is unless your team members are extremely shy and aren't comfortable with public accolades.

  Even if you can make your own decisions, you should try and involve your employees in a discussion in case they give you a new point of view from where to approach your tasks. Then there will be the added benefit of your employee getting their mind off from work in order to engage in something they feel that will benefit the company, this will result in their mind getting a well-needed reprieve from continuous work so when they finally get back to work, their mind will be refreshed and their energy will be somewhat replenished so they will be able to focus on a task better than before. More than that, they'll feel that you really value what they have to say, which makes them feel very good about themselves and the work that they do. You're able to hit to birds with one stone: more ideas and a more motivated team member.

- **Show Empathy:**

  You're not the only one who's human – your employees are too. As such, they are also very complex creatures. This means they're dynamic in the sense that every day, they might be feeling something new or dealing with a new set of problems. What may work for them today may not necessarily work for them tomorrow. There may be times that though work longer hours, their productivity doesn't increase as their minds may not be in their work completely. This is a natural occurrence but one that can be prevented easily by showing empathy towards your employees. Ask them questions if they look worried or stressed out in a manner that sounds more concerned about their welfare than about their productivity.

  A female employee might be worried about leaving her children without a babysitter. A young employee might be having trouble managing time with their assignments or exams and work. Although these problems don't directly affect you, they affect the work you will be getting so inevitably, it will affect you as a manager. So it is better to approach employees at the first time of trouble rather than having them redo their work that will only cause frustration and will cause them to lose time. Prevention or early intervention is definitely much better than any potent cure.

Encourage your employee to come up to you if they have a problem that they feel you might be able to help them with. Not only will you help them feel better, you'll also be able to earn more of their trust and respect.

- **Make Their Work Easier:**

  If you expect your team members to be more productive, be sure you do your part by helping them become so. Aside from fostering an environment conducive to higher productivity, give them the tools for it too.

  Don't waste your employees' times by giving them equipment that is slow, broken or outdated. In a professional environment, everything needs to be efficient. If your employee has to wait three minutes for a document to save, they will lose their train of thought. If you want your team members to be able to process 5 transactions every 15 minutes, make sure that the equipment they use can actually process at least 5 transactions every quarter of an hour. It's useless to motivate them to do so when they're using outmoded computers that can process at most 2 transactions per quarter of an hour.

  Make sure that everything from the computer you provide to the photocopier is working at optimum speed. Requiring more from the without the necessary equipment that'll enable them to perform as well as you'd like them too won't just erode your integrity with them, it'll also give them excuses to slack off just using your inability to provide the adequate equipment as such. If you feel that your office is lagging behind in the latest technology and your organization can afford it, order new and more efficient equipment. If it's not immediately possible, start off with replacing the most crucial items first but make sure that everything in your office is working at an efficiency rate at which you would want your employees to work: quickly and without delay. Otherwise, you may want to postpone requiring a higher level of productivity from your team until the proper equipment arrives.

- **Encourage Questions:**

  Usually, an employee will believe that they have to solve all their problems themselves and if they don't, they're screwed. This will mean that even in the occasion where they need more power and more experience, they will try to answer their own queries to the best of their knowledge either by second guessing how to do whatever it is they believe they need to finish on their own or by having to research it themselves. This can lead to wastage of time and resources because both ways of finding out how to do what they need to do takes time away from actual work and the risk is high that whatever it is they discover may not be the appropriate course of action or method.

  You can minimize this risk by encouraging your employees to ask questions. When they know that you're ok with the fact that they don't know everything and that they can come up to you and simply ask without being judged as incompetent, they won't even bother taking that risk of finding out themselves. In every meeting, at the beginning of every day, try and encourage your employees to ask a question about their work. Tell them that if for some reason they don't want to ask questions now, they can always do so later. Oh, and it's also important how you ask them, i.e., the tone of voice and body language. If your tone of voice and facial expression screams that it's not ok to not know everything, no amount of guaranteeing and asking will work.

Gently and pleasantly "drill" the point into their heads that asking questions is a good thing and it will help them increase their productivity as well. Tell them the different advantages and benefits of doing so. For example, that they can cut their working time significantly if they ask the right questions.

When an employee does ask a question, welcome them not just with your words but most especially – as noted earlier – through your tone of voice and body language. Don't' make them feel like you are being burdened because this will discourage them and others from ever approaching you again which will cause productivity to plummet.

- **Celebrate Your Tasks:**

  A great way to spur your team to continuously achieve challenging milestones and perform well is by celebrating important accomplishments. If you manage to secure a difficult client, celebrate. If you manage to complete a task, celebrate. After every major job well done, give your team members a bit of a treat, even if it means giving them half the day off. This is an inexpensive way to show your employees that you appreciate them working and value their hard work in your own way. Remember that when your team members are feel well appreciated and highly motivated, you need very little prodding for them to always give excellent work.

Not every company can afford to reward employees every time so even just giving a well-done speech will show your employees that though the time might not be ripe to open the champagne, you are still taking in their hard work and would want to reward it somewhat substantially in the future.

Just remember to be, as Dale Carnegie (famous success guru and author of the classic and current bestselling book How To Win Friends And Influence People), hearty in approbation and lavish in praise and you'll have a motivated and accomplished team in your hands.

- **Be the Leader:**

  Again, with the one point that has been emphasized time and time again throughout this book - you are the leader; what you do, others will follow. One critical implication of this is that the person you will have to monitor the strictest is, surprise, yourself. As action speaks louder than words, the way you conduct yourself is the best (or worst?) preaching that your team members will follow by heart. When there's a conflict between between what you say and do, guess who usually wins? That's right – actions. To be an effective leader, integrity is very, very important.

  If for example, you are a habitual latecomer, your employees will consider it their right to be tardy. In their minds, they'll say if you as leader can't come to work on time, what more they who are lesser mortals than you. If you slack off at work, your employees will be one step ahead of you and believe you don't have the right to expect something that you yourself can't give. If, however, you are a model employee yourself, your team will feel that they have to work as hard as you do, if not harder than you. When you practice what you preach, you tell show them what you're asking for in terms of quality of and attitude in work is not out-of-this-world but rather, they're practical. When you act with integrity, i.e., your actions equal or exceed your words, you establish your leadership authority that they can't help but acknowledge and follow.

Remember that just like children look up to a teacher, your team will look up to you. This is a good opportunity for any manager to bring his team on track because this means that even the employees who have lost their train and have lagged behind can motivate themselves by looking up to you. Hence, if there is nothing else you can do, start doing your own work the way you would like them to do theirs. As a famous line from a famous religious figure goes, do unto others what you want them to do unto you.

- **Debunk the Myth of the Favorites:**

  Although it has been said that we should treat others equitably instead of equally, it doesn't mean equal treatment is something to be shunned at work and members of your team should be treated based on their situation and needs. No, you'll still need to treat them equally in certain areas, especially when it comes to office rules, regulations, policies and guidelines. In this regard, you as a manager should never have favorites to begin with. Never make it seem like you prefer one employee to another, even if you do, by implementing office regulations differently from one member to another. If you do, you'll give your team members the impression that you have favorites and this might cause division among your team members where the not-favorites may turn against the chosen ones by, among other things, slacking off on their own jobs due to feeling underappreciated. This will cause work to slow down considerably.

Let's face it: you'll look more favorably on some team members than others. It's normal because some will have a much better work attitude than others, among other things. But it's not an excuse to show favoritism. Force yourself, if need be, to interact with your least favorite team members too and assign them tasks. Talk to them. Interact with everyone as much as you do with your favorite employee. Make everyone feel equally appreciated but still not superhuman enough to get away with being lazy. Drill this fact into everyone's mind including your own that your first priority is the office and that personal work productivity is the only basis for accolades and rewards.

It is not hard to encourage your employees to make more progress or to boost their productivity. Remember that every day you will have the opportunity to make a network with each and every one of your teammates. You need to utilize this opportunity to boost your employees' productivity and make them feel more secure in the office environment. A happy employee is the product of a healthy environment and even though you might be a superb manager, you will need your team to build your company. Hence, invest in your tools and hone them for the best results possible.

Chapter 9

How to Bridge the Gap between Upper Management and Your Team

Sadly, it is a fact that due to some elements, there is a bit of a communication gap between upper management and your team. It's normal. However, as a manager, it is your job to act as a bridge between these two sides of the lake – minimize the gap so to speak – in order for communications to start flowing well. Consider yourself a mediator – a high priest so to speak – between the gods-that-be that's upper management and ordinary mortals that are your team members. Remember, being one in team spirit shouldn't just be limited to your immediate team. It should also extend to the whole organization in general and for your team members, the organization is represented by upper management.

An effective manager is a great bridge because he is aware of both the teams' sentiments. This is because he is half-and-half, not in a dairy kind of sense but in terms of having one foot of his or her mind inside the upper management's team and the other foot inside your own team. You have the privilege of knowing the sentiments of both sides and to a great extent, know their needs and how to best approach them. Knowing these sentiments, however, is not enough. You can either continue merely relaying information to both sides or you can build a system into which everyone fits comfortably so the conversation keeps flowing and you're able to minimize the gap enough to enable both upper management and your team members to work together well, being of similar minds and directions.

Here are a few ways to significantly improve communication lines between upper management and your own team members, minimize the communication gaps and align your members' hearts and mind as much as possible with the organization's:

Open-Door Communication Policies:

This means giving everyone – whether upper management or your team members – the chance to be heard by the other side. Doing so can help build a sense of trust, oneness and respect between the two parties. This is the best and easiest way to get communication going since both sides willingly show their cards and give feedback. If members of both sides are reluctant to communicate in public, gather feedback from both sides via less personal or public means such as email and communicate it to the other side so that every side knows what they're doing, what they need to do and what they need to stop doing.

The biggest benefit of open-door communication policies is it can help build trust and respect between the two sides, both of which are important if both parties are to work together well. I remember two instances in one of the companies I used to work for where one president was too aloof to mingle with us mere mortals while another one had an open-door communications policy. The aloof president always maintained that to communicate with him, you need to go through several layers of upper management so by the time lower management's messages or concerns got to him, if ever they did, they were already watered down. As such, the aloof president didn't show any concern for our needs and issues. The result is a strained relationship between management and staff that kept the company from effectively addressing key issues quickly.

Contrast it to the other president, Mr. Popular. He never failed to visit each and every department towards the end of every business day, encouraged the people to go home on time so they can spend time with their families and allowed direct access to his office – at least through the union representatives. Because of such an open line of communications, he's able to effectively assess the needs of employees in general, act on them well, earn their trust and respect, and was able to create an atmosphere where in management and employees work together well and were able to address key company issues effectively and promptly.

That's the power of an open door policy. But this isn't a perfect one. One drawback, if overdone and not managed well, can lead to employees or their representatives overstepping their bounds and become too comfortable. Granting open access but limiting it to key representatives can help mitigate this risk.

Meet!

Holding meetings is crucial. Usually, both sides are completely unaware of who is on the other side. Introduce your team to the management and vice versa. Make it known who is responsible for what and highlight each side's achievements. Then, give everyone the platform to discuss any issue that they might have with the other side and also have them provide at least one solution to the issue they might have.

Meetings give both sides the opportunities to interact and see the "human" sides of each other. Usually, each side views the other not as people but as obligations. When both sides meet at the right frequency, real relationships develop that help the organization run like a well-oiled machine.

Just make sure to limit both the frequency and durations of meetings. Too frequent meetings run the risk of wasting company time and resources because some items on the agenda can actually be addressed via email, which can significantly save much needed time and resources for more important stuff. Set or conduct meetings only for those things that really need to be discussed sitting down face to face for efficient use of company time and resources.

Also, try to keep your meetings short – 30 minutes is a good target to aim for. The tendency for most meetings is to veer too far away from the main points in the agenda and inadvertently drag on for hours with very little going by the way of accomplishments. One of the reasons for this is lack of preparation. To remedy this, it's best that all necessary information for decision-making be furnished to everyone attending the meeting at least 1 day before the meeting. This gives members the opportunity to already think about and process the issues that need to be resolved during meetings prior to them. When they come to the meeting, members will no longer have to study and analyze the issues during meetings, they'll be able to significantly reduce the amount of time needed for discussion and brainstorming of ideas and can accomplish what needs to be accomplished as quickly as possible. Meetings that end on time or even earlier tend to be more productive than meetings that drag on forever.

Recognize Your Team's Body Language:

It's been said that effective communications are only 10% verbal and 90% non-verbal. This is why the saying that actions speak louder than words hold much water. There will be times that your team members' words will not reflect what they are really trying to say. They may say "yes" but their body language reveals a resounding "no" and they may say they can but their body language reveals they doubt their own abilities to get the job done. To the extent you're able to read your members' body language is the extent you'll be able to effectively assess situations and act accordingly.

You will notice when your team is uncomfortable with something. Recognize their body language and have them tell you what's on their mind. Also recognize their style of work. Some might be silent workers whilst others might be leaders. It is your job to get everyone to discuss his or her reservations without someone being left out or bullied. If you feel that one member is being targeted, stop the bullying and assure everyone that his or her issue will be resolved.

When you're able to effectively assess your own team's situation, you can give management better feedback and give them the opportunity to address your team's issues and strengthen the bond between the two parties.

Note The Feedback:

Believe me, it's practically impossible to take in every important detail during meetings. You'll tend to focus on what you believe to be important and in the process, zone out of other details that may seem mundane at the time but may actually be crucial to your decision making later on. So how can you get the most details out of your meetings?

Make notes or record the meeting. Take minutes if you have to but make sure that when you meet the next time, no one can point out the same issues about your team. By recording your meetings, you'll have the opportunity to accurately go back to important details that you may have missed, which can prove to be important later on.

Also, help the other management improve themselves. As a manager, it is your job to create harmony between both the sides. Take each and every member aside and assign tasks that help him or her get better at what they are required to do. In the next meeting, make sure to highlight the team member's improvement. Make it known as much as the issue was raised so your member's morale is boosted once more and they work harder and more efficiently.

Remember, the more details you get from meetings, the more information you'll be able to process and provide to upper management and help them make good decisions and consequently, tighten the bond between them and your team.

Open Doors:

Open doors that even while you're not around, the gates remain open and members may talk to upper management freely. Communication helps resolve a lot of issues. This is one of the most beneficial things you can do since it will help resolve a lot of issues under the table. One exercise is to give each member of the table a copy of everyone's email address so whenever someone has an issue, they can take it up with the person who is responsible. This will increase conversation and also cause an overall friendly atmosphere to permeate the environment.

Monitor Performance:

More than planning and implementing, plans or courses of action need to be monitored. Otherwise, how will you or upper management know if such courses of action are effective or need to be adjusted or replaced altogether? Only by monitoring performance will you be able to help upper management effectively manage the organization towards continuing success.

Every meeting should be at least a month apart. This will give everyone ample time to make up on what they lack. However, this month should not go by in silence. If you assign someone a task to improve, keep a check on that. Even if you don't, keep yourself updated with what they're doing regarding their particular issue. This will mean that your employees as well as upper management will be both under the impression that their issue is serious and hence they will make an effort to work on it.

When it comes to being able to effectively monitor performance, communications is key. Most information gaps are actually communication gaps and as such, free-flowing communication will greatly help minimize your and the upper management team's communication gap. With more information available, you can help upper management make better decisions. Remember yourself and remind everyone that at the end of the day, everyone is a human dealing with their own issues and problems and no one has more power over anyone else, no matter what their status in the office.

This will help upper management accept the employees as people of their own and it will help dissolve any apprehensions the employees might have about interacting as well.

Furthermore, it is always a good idea to have team activities conducted. If you feel that after multiple meetings, you are still at a block, you can always opt for such activities where you divide employees and upper management in groups that have issues with each other. The more they get to know each other, the better they will resolve their issues and the better the communication will start to flow.

As a manager, it will be expected of you to keep feedback from both sides flowing but a smart manager knows that systems are better than individuals; hence it will be in your benefit and everyone else's that you keep conversation flowing in an automatic way so you only have to intervene when absolutely necessary.

Doing so will not only take the burden off your shoulders but it will also help you make a reputation as a smart, effective and remarkable manager. As a manager, the best thing you can do is build a network where everything runs smoothly like a well-oiled machine.

Hence, be smart and start at the base of the problem. Then, build your communication platform up reaching higher management. Bring everyone to the table, give your presentation, start the conversation going and stand back and only intervene here and there when you feel that things are getting off track and you will be good to go.

Ross Elkins

Chapter 10

Management Tips for a New Manager

It can be quite challenging managing a team, more so if it's your first time to do so. Chances are, you're probably very excited about your job and feel a good mix of emotions, i.e., nervously positive and excited.

Such positions, however, come with a lot of responsibilities that lead to a lot of apprehensions. Additionally, there is always the fear of making false starts. If you have any such apprehensions, here is a list of tips that will help you to excel in your field:

- **Don't Get in Over your Head:**

   Remember your employee days – especially the important lessons – and remember them well. Try to recall your own previous managers' booboos, including how and why they happened. This will help you avoid making the same mistakes as a manager and minimize the risk of screwing so many things up as a rookie.

   In particular, learn from your previous managers' mistakes in handling the team. Remember, you're not the

Grand Dictator of the empire and acting as such will only cause your employees to either be demotivated to work excellently under your watch or provoke them to actually sabotaging the team by deliberately working poorly. Remember that you will attract more flies with honey than with vinegar and don't push anyone around solely because you have the power to do so. Keep a level head and be confidently humble.

- **Be Confident:**

You may think it's impossible to be confident about being a new manager considering it's your first time handling people. While that may be true to some extent, remember that handling people is only part of the job. Your superiors wouldn't have promoted you to that position if they didn't think you're up to to the task. In which case, you can be confident enough to handle the job knowing that the people that really know if you're cut out for the job or not – upper management – believe that you are. 'Nuff said.

You need to be confident because if you're not, several not-so-good things can happen. First, your team members may overstep their boundaries and push you around – control you even. When they see you're unsure of your actions and decisions and that you're afraid of them, they be like sharks and smell blood – they'll go in for the kill! When they do, you lose control and influence over your team members and you may eventually have to be replaced by – of all people – one of your team members.

Secondly, lack of confidence leads to poorly made and executed decisions. Either you'll make the wrong decisions out of peer pressure or won't be able to execute them well in the face of resistance from your members. Either way, it'll still lead to you becoming an ineffective manager that may ultimately cost you your job and your ego.

So be confident because your superiors are in your abilities and talents. Don't let them down.

- **Ask Your Boss (Current Or Former) For Advice:**

You don't have to reinvent the wheel. I mean, why wrack your brain open trying to address important issues effectively if your predecessors have already done it for you when they encountered the same during their tenure? There is no one better to ask for advice than someone who's worn your shoes. Your boss will know exactly how tough your job is and if there's ever a good time to learn from their pool of wisdom, it is now.

There's no shame in admitting you don't know everything or in asking for help, especially from someone who's more experienced than you. The real shame is in failing because you were too proud to ask. So go ahead, ask questions. Ask them about the mistakes they made and try to learn from them so that you don't repeat them. There will be a lot of points they will make that you might not like but at the end, you will find both, points to keep and points to let go. Hence, it is always good to discuss.

Just a word of caution when asking your boss for advice, you shouldn't just take everything they say as gospel truth. Do some critical thinking and evaluation yourself before deciding to accept them. There may be times that because of differences in situations, you may need to either modify or reject their advice. Yes, it's good to ask but it's also good to think about your boss' answer to your questions.

- **Learn About Your Organization:**

There will be some things that you will have to do according to your organization. Remember that as a manager, you're not the owner but a steward of the owners' resources. You need to align yourself with the owners' mission, vision and priorities and as such, you'll need to learn as much as you can about your organization.

One of the best ways to easily do this is through clear and open communications with upper management. If you're the bridge between your team members and upper management, the latter is the bridge between you and the owners. By strictly adhering to your superiors' instructions as much as possible, you'll be able to indirectly learn about your organization and act in line with its core values and priorities.

Another way is to ask your superiors and do some research on your organization's history and other important information about it. Memorize these before you start to work. Don't be afraid to adapt. Failing to do so can cost you your job or get you labeled as a stubborn and ineffective manager. Remember to keep your principles close and to incorporate them with those that the organization values. Institutions run on the same principles for decades and centuries. Hence why it is very important to learn the culture of where you're performing.

- **Find And Emulate A Role Model:**

There's a reason why many successful personalities have a huge cult following trying to copy their every move: they do what normally works and brings massive success. That's why you see so many people dressing like, playing like and talking like their favorite athletes, thinking there's some magical potion to the latter's fashion, playing style and manner of speaking. To some extent, it helps the fans succeed faster because they no longer have to figure out what works – their favorite celebrity athletes already did and all they need to do is use the same formula.

Throughout your employee career, there might have been a manager you preferred over all others – your "celebrity athlete" so to speak. Ponder and think hard over what it was that made them successful. As an employee start to remember what you wanted, what your manager delivered and what allowed them to experience lasting success. Again, you don't have to reinvent the wheel as much as you think you need to. Build on what was already built on by your role model and proceed to improve from there.

- **Make Friends:**

  A good manager is friendly, not aloof. Harsh managers are unreachable and though they might get things done, they can't maintain it for long. It won't be long before their team members launch a coup or an uprising that will either topple them directly or indirectly by performing poorly and having upper management fire or reassign him or her to another team.

  On the other hand, a good manager is one who is friendly and cares for his team. Don't burden someone like you were burdened yourself. Hold a lot of meetings that let you know your team and get your team to know each other as well. A friendly environment is the best for productivity. Your single biggest asset as a manager is your team members' unwavering commitment and support and without which, you're doomed.

- **Don't Make Enemies:**

A good manager understands that people come from different places and hence different people will have differences. As manager, it's your responsibility to make sure these differences don't get in the way of team members' working relationships and team productivity. The key to this the previous point: make friends with your team members. When you develop a good working relationship with them, you get their respect, trust and commitment that will enable them to work past whatever differences they may have with other team members.

- **Ask Your Team:**

The best way to minimize mistakes is to anticipate what may work or may not work. If you're a new manager, you don't have the benefit of experience to draw such ideas from. So what are you to do? Since you already considered asking your previous bosses and identifying and emulating a role model, it's time to consider the opinion of your subordinates – the people you'll be directly responsible for in terms of managing and leading.

On your first week, ask your staff what they think is a good manager. You will find some unrealistic expectations but also some practical ones that will help you become a good manager if not a perfect one. Remember that you do not have to be perfect but you will only get ninety percent if you strive for the full hundred.

Your team might have worked with someone in the past. Ask them to compare yourself with your predecessor and what they did right and what they wish you wouldn't repeat. If you find some habits that are nice, keep them. Let go of unnecessary ones that might give your team a needlessly tough time. Remember that though you are an authority, you need to be compassionate in order to be effective. A team that helps you become your full potential is an asset and it would be foolishness not to utilize the help you're getting.

So always keep trying to look for feedback in order to improve yourself. And as with asking your previous bosses, don't just take what they say at face value. Think about and evaluate them in order to see if they're workable or realistic. Accept those that are and discard those that are ludicrous or unrealistic.

- **Talk to Others Who Applied for Your Position:**

  You might now be in a place where others strived to be. Don't alienate someone and try to be friendly with anyone who strived for your position. Ask questions about what you can do to be a good manager in their opinion. Ask if they would like you to carry a tradition or eliminate a bad habit. You will get your best feedback from your worst critics.

- **Identify Your Goals:**

You may have already gotten feedback as to what a good manager looks like from the points of view of your previous bosses, identified role models and your team members. It's now time to consider what your ideas of a good manager are by identifying your goals as manager.

As a manager, your job is to achieve goals. Identify these and make a list. Remember, the primary way that you'll be judged as an effective or ineffective manager is by your ability to achieve goals and you won't be able to achieve them without first identifying the right ones. After which, prioritize the goals that need attention first and start working on them in order to have place to start off from.

Aside from not having any idea of how to become an effective manager, failing to identify your goals will mean that you will never know where to begin. When you make a goal, you make a priority. Thus, work for your priorities. If you fail to do this, you will likely pull from a stack and the whole empire will come crashing down on top of you.

If you find that you don't yet have an ultimate goal, create short-term goals such as, in one month, three months, six months, one year, five years, ten years, etc. I want to be here. Doing so will help you realize where you want to be in the end. This will also help you work harder and more efficiently like a racer who runs harder when he sees the finish line.

- **Don't Stress:**

This is one of the most common mistakes a manager will make. Don't let the position terrify you enough that you lose track of what you're doing. Remember that you do you remarkably well and someone chose you for a very good reason. Hence, remember to take deep breaths and occasional breaks. Relax for short periods of time and reflect on how to improve yourself, your life and your managerial skills.

A person at rest is a person that can be at his or her best.

Ross Elkins

Chapter 11

The Qualities of an Effective Manager

As a manager, your work will take up a large portion of your life. This means that you will have to balance your work and personal life at more occasions than one. Since, the purpose of this book is to train and hone you completely; we feel that this topic is as important as any other that is discussed in this book.

What Happens When You Don't Balance Your Work And Personal Life?

Have you ever ridden a bicycle? By that I mean 2 wheels and with no "balancers". Have you noticed that in order for you to get to where you're going, you'll need to be able to balance yourself on the bike? Further, didn't you also notice that the better your balance is, the faster you can go – even on the sharp curves?

It's the same with your personal productivity as a manager. Your ability to balance the bicycle that's your life will determine how fast and far you can go in life, including your career as a manager. Chronic work-life imbalance won't just slow you down, it can also cause you to fail altogether. Hence, you'll need to maintain well-balanced life.

There's a saying about how failing to plan is equivalent to planning to fail, albeit unconsciously. As a manager, your job is to plan and handle tasks. If you fail to plan your own life, as is the case with work, your life will turn into utter chaos. As such, your personal concerns will eventually seep into your work and significantly affect your managerial performance. You will find yourself both burning out without even accomplish anything significant. This in turn will make your personal life even more of a living hell that will also affect your career and eventually becomes a downward spiral from which you may have a very hard time climbing out of.

So, if you feel that both your lives have lately been spiraling out of control, or rather, have been bleeding into each other in a way that is concerning for you, be sure to consult this chapter and learn or even re-learn how to keep both your lives separate so you work to your full potential without burning out!

- **Set Your Priorities:**

    Balance is primarily dependent on knowing what are the things you'll need to put on a balancing platform like a scale, which is your life. This "things" are called priorities and identifying these is very important in terms of creating a good work-life balance.

    Success means different things to different people. When you have identified what you consider to be success, you'll be able to identify the right priorities. Without a clear personal definition of what success means for your, you won't be able to identify the things you'll need to focus on.

Ask yourself if you could only focus on one thing for the rest of your life, what that would be. This answer, typically, is your first priority. Some people believe money, power and fame should be their life's focus while others who are more altruistic believe it should be helping the poor, saving the environment or propagating their religion. Keep at it until you have a list.

When you already have a list of what you believe are the things you should focus your life on, trim it down. After much evaluation, remove anything that you find that is unnecessary to both your personal as well as professional life. Learn to de-clutter your life whilst focusing on your priorities. While it's very important to identify what you want to focus on, too may items on your list will spread you too thin to effectively do well in any of those items.

Consider sunlight. In and by itself, it's scattered and won't be able to burn a hole through paper. But use a magnifying glass to narrow it down and focus it, it becomes powerful enough to burn a hole and even start a fire. That's the power of focus and that's why you'll need to keep your priorities limited to just the few really important ones.

This will help you to remain focused as well as happy. When you work on something that is your highest priority, you will naturally work with increased levels of interest and enthusiasm. Hence, make a list of priorities and start working on what most closely affects you. Keep in mind that even if you don't like your first priority, it is what needs to be done first and foremost. Training your brain like this will keep you from lagging and you will complete your task easily and quickly.

- **Time Management**

Remember all those track-team races? Remember how all you wanted to do was to beat the whistle in record time? When you work on restoring balance to your life, you will realize that you will find yourself in situations similar to a track-team race. You will have to meet deadlines, appear in meetings and do everything in a given amount of time. However, all this will not be possible until you are giving your best.

Hence, even when you don't have a clock ticking on your head, it is always a good idea to time yourself and see how quickly you can complete your tasks. This does not meant reaching your office in record time after you've overslept but in fact, timing yourself to see how long it takes for you to complete the first mile on your morning jog. Get a stopwatch and see how quickly it takes for you to make an assignment. See how quickly you can gather all the information you need in order to tackle a certain task.

Hence, start timing yourself and see how many minutes you waste that you could have saved. By doing this, you complete tasks efficiently and with increased levels of focus. Also, the time you save, at the end of the day, can be spent in pleasurable activities to help you relax.

Doing this consistently will help you become more and more efficient in managing your time and in effect, "creating" more time for improving work-life balance and overall personal productivity.

- **Focus is Key:**

  So many times, you will find yourself tempted to do everything at once. This is an illusion. Multitasking is best done by computers, not humans. Yes, people may get away with multi-tasking but they aren't able to maximize their productivity – at least the quality of their work.

  Multi-tasking runs the risk of missing out on key details that can make or break your projects. If that isn't the case, then why is it surgeons need to operate in a room that's orderly and quiet? If a surgeon operates on your heart or brain in a noisy and chaotic operating room, he may be distracted and may accidentally cut something that shouldn't be and botch the whole operation.

  You don't need to be a surgeon to appreciate the need for focus. As a manager, you need to be just as focused and precise as a surgeon. Some mistakes due to carelessness can lead to significant financial losses for your organization. It can also cost you your job.

  Keep in mind the fact that when you give everything your five percent instead of giving one thing your hundred percent, you start losing efficiency. You will never be able to focus on the task at hand because your mind will be jumping to the immediately next task.

  Doing this will not only take your focus away from work completely, it will also give you added levels of stress and stress cannot only be cured by simple sleep.

Hence, if you find yourself with your focus deviating, consult the list you prepared in point one and start working on whatever comes first. No matter how pressing other tasks may seem, they can almost always wait. Plus, when you focus on one task, you complete it efficiently instead of letting all your tasks hanging, which will happen if you try and do everything all at once.

- **Make Room For Fun:**

The other half of work-life balance is, well, life! You'll need to enjoy enough fun activities and experiences in life in order to maintain optimal work performance and productivity. So go ahead, tap into your inner child and do things that you enjoy every now and then. Don't try to think mature – play video games and other seemingly childish activities if they give you pleasure and fun. There's no rule prohibiting adults from enjoying youthful fun.

Personally, I play my favorite video games on my android smartphone for 5 minutes after every 25-minute working period. Prior to doing this, I used to try and work for hours on end without taking fun breaks and I eventually burned out. After I started incorporating these fun 5-minutes playing breaks (better known as the Pomodoro technique), I found myself able to work for longer with increased focus. The frequent 5-minute playing breaks are fun for me and helped me extend my peak mental performance at work.

Be creative and you could actually include this in your work as well, only when permissible. You can also incorporate fun breaks in a different way, such as going to your favorite food place for lunch or hitting the gym on lunch breaks.

These tasks also don't have to be over-the-top. If you look forward to listening to music whilst working, invest in a pair of headphones you can whip out whenever you find yourself working alone. Try and indulge in something that takes your mind off the mundane. Not every task and assignment will be as challenging and exciting as you want it to be. Indeed, these will make you feel like you aren't achieving to your full potential when that won't be true. Hence, to keep a positive outlook on life, have some fun while you work.

The important thing is to incorporate as much fun activities in between work as much as optimally possible for continuous and extended personal productivity.

- **Respect Your Me-Time:**

  True, no man or woman is an island. But hey, everyone needs some alone time every now and then to unclutter the mind, relax and refocus. Without this, you may feel a constant sense of being overwhelmed and lose sight of what's really important and where you're heading personally and in your career.

  Designating regular "me" times and keeping them sacred will go a long way towards helping you become and stay an effective manager.

  Pick up any book on success and you will note that this is a point that all the greats have got down pat. If it is time to relax, relax you shall. For a certain amount of time a day, even if it is no more than an hour, set aside work completely. Clear your mind and focus on yourself. This doesn't mean spending an hour in front of the TV, though that may seem therapeutic to some.

For one hour a day, turn your phone to silent and relax. Take a long bath; pamper yourself. Indulge in some exercise or best of all: do yoga. Even by sitting in the lotus position, you will find that your muscles seem looser and your stress will gradually lessen over time. Whatever you do, do it consistently and no matter what, do not let work or anything else interfere in your 'me-time'. If you start working full-time, you will feel like a machine that hasn't been oiled in some time. You will feel strained and as if your brain is burning out. So, in order to avoid this, find some time to relax, even if just for the added productivity.

- **Step Back And See:**

  Regular self-assessment and reflection is a very important aspect of creating and maintaining a great work-life balance. This way, you're able to see if you're still on track in terms of your goals and priorities or if you've deviated and are veering further away from them, in which case you get the opportunity to get back on track.

  Once in a while, put down your pen and step back and see yourself from an outsider's perspective. Make a list of all the bad habits you have. Poor sleep cycle, bad eating habits and poor exercise patterns might be a few of the major things you will find on your list. If you have the benefit of asking feedback from others, take advantage of it by asking them. As much as you try to look at yourself from an outsider's perspective, there'll be times when you won't be able to objectively do so.

Now, after each item, write the consequence of this habit. This practice is not meant to scare you and make you even more stressed, in fact, it will help you kick these habits. Like when you show a smoker the effects of smoking on the human body, this exercise is meant to show you what your seemingly harmless habits of carelessness are doing to your body.

Once you've made this list, you will find that every time you pick up something unhealthy to eat, you will be thinking twice. You will also find yourself making room for more sleep. Also, you will find that even if you can't devote hours to the gym, your body will try and remain active in other ways even if it means walking home from work instead of taking the bus.

- **Take A Vacation:**

    Many people, especially very career-driven people, make the mistake of believing that their careers are the be-all and end-all of their existence and as such, they worship their careers like gods and dedicate as much of their waking hours to them. To them, taking vacations are a waste of time and money. Some even view them as the devil incarnate!

    Such a belief is probably the single most formidable enemy of a good work-life balance. A manager, especially a young one, will believe that they are somewhat invincible and that nothing can hinder their performance. This is simply not true. Even though you might write off your own stress, your body is taking a major toll. This will affect your productivity and will cause you to slow down. As a result, your work will suffer majorly.

Hence, even if it means going away for no more than a weekend, take a vacation, turn off your cellphone, forget your laptop and relax. Try not to 'relax' by doing work-related activities because though you might be relaxing, you will be slacking off even at that. Instead, go swimming; maybe spend a day at the sauna, getting a massage to relax your inevitably sore and overworked muscles; or even just read a book in bed. Whatever you do, remember that just like your me-time, this time is meant to be for relaxing. So even if you would like nothing more than to catch up on sleep, indulge in an activity that you like enough to do it without the regret of wasting your time.

By taking regular time off from work, you're able to recharge, recover and recuperate well and come back to work more energized and productive.

- **Spend Time With People:**

Work has a way of taking you away from the people who aren't immediately connected to work but are very important to you personally. Go through your cell-phone's log and you'll only find a list of employees and business-related calls in the log. It may not be so obvious but believe me, not spending enough time with non-work people such as family, friends or hobby groups can seriously tilt your life scale more towards work and result in a very imbalanced life.

Hit up an old friend, talk to your family or your significant other. If you find that you don't want to talk to anyone like that, join a club. Visit a gym or even the park. Anything that can provide you the opportunity to get as much non-work human interaction as you can for maintaining a good work-life balance. You'll appreciate people from work even more when you do.

- **Set Boundaries and Respect Them:**

  In today's very high tech and "wired" society, people are so much more connected with each other in ways that were unimaginable merely one or two generations ago. But this doesn't come without cost: privacy. Gone are the days you can go home and really feel like you're away from work. As a manager, chances are that your organization will issue you gadgets to make sure you're accessible 24/7 – even while on vacation. I've known people who get away to other countries for a vacation only to find that they still work while on a holiday trip because of today's high tech communications.

  As such, you'll need to actively set boundaries and limits to your privacy. For example, tell your subordinates and superiors not to contact you on your off hours unless it's absolutely urgent and critical. One way to encourage this is delegate more things to your team members and give them authority to take care of certain things so that you minimize disruptions on your private time.

  Tim Ferris, best selling author of The 4-Hour Workweek suggests that to the extent possible, set specific times to check and answer emails within the day and stick to it.

Over time, you condition people to expect that you're not as easily reachable and will thus make sure to make the most out of their limited contact with you. He also does the same for phone calls, when possible.

Also, try to make a timetable if it helps. Devote times to work and pleasure with some time for relaxation other than sleep. Don't be alarmed if you find yourself allocating more than eight hours of work. There is nothing wrong with wanting to work more. However, when that work begins to seep into your sleep and relaxation, even the time you eat, that is very alarming and unhealthy because it means that you are setting yourself down the path of destruction. Learn to set your boundaries and respect them like you would any other person's.

By setting boundaries and training people to respect them, you're able to have more privacy and "me" times towards a good work-life balance.

- **Find Your Crowd:**

  If you find that you are still in need of some help, find other managers and discuss how you could help balance your work and life in such a way that nothing suffers. People who have been in the field longer than you will have a lot of insight to offer. Even a new manager might give you something to think about that you might not have thought about yourself. Hence, talk to other people about your problems and not only will they look more realistic to solve, you will also find an easy solution too.

Chapter 12

Work/Life Management-The Precarious Balance Between Your Two Lives

As a manager, your work will take up a large portion of your life. This means that you will have to balance your work and personal life at more occasions than one. Since, the purpose of this book is to train and hone you completely; we feel that this topic is as important as any other that is discussed in this book.

What Happens When You Don't Balance Your Work And Personal Life?

It all comes down to planning. As a manager, your job is to plan and handle tasks. If you fail to plan your own life, as is the case with work, your life will turn into utter chaos. You will find yourself both burning out whilst you don't even accomplish anything. This will lead to unhealthy levels of stress, unhappiness and your biggest fear: reduced productivity.

So, if you feel that both your lives have lately been spiraling out of control, or rather, have been bleeding into each other in a way that is concerning for you, be sure to consult this chapter and learn or even re-learn how to keep both your lives separate so you work to your full potential without burning out!

- **Set Your Priorities:**

This is the first and foremost task to achieving balance. Success means different things to different people. Yes, everyone aims for the moon in their own way but while one thing may be a goal to some people, to others, it might be simply, a milestone.

Ask yourself if you could only focus on one thing for the rest of your life, what that would be. This answer, typically, is your first priority. Keep doing this until you have a list. Then, if possible, cut off anything that you find that is unnecessary to both your personal as well as professional life. Learn to de-clutter your life whilst focusing on your priorities.

This will help you to remain focused as well as happy. When you work on something that is your highest priority, you will naturally work with increased levels of interest and enthusiasm. Hence, make a list of priorities and start working on what most closely affects you. Keep in mind that even if you don't like your first priority, it is what needs to be done first and foremost. Training your brain like this will keep you from lagging and you will complete your task easily and quickly.

- **Back To School!**

Remember all those track-team races? Remember how all you wanted to do was to beat the whistle in record time? When you work on restoring balance to your life, you will realize that you will find yourself in situations similar to a track-team race. You will have to meet deadlines, appear in meetings and do everything in a given amount of time. However, all this will not be possible until you are giving your best.

Hence, even when you don't have a clock ticking on your head, it is always a good idea to time yourself and see how quickly you can complete your tasks. This does not meant reaching your office in record time after you've overslept but in fact, timing yourself to see how long it takes for you to complete the first mile on your morning jog. Get a stopwatch and see how quickly it takes for you to make an assignment. See how quickly you can gather all the information you need in order to tackle a certain task.

Hence, start timing yourself and see how many minutes you waste that you could have saved. By doing this, you complete tasks efficiently and with increased levels of focus. Also, the time you save, at the end of the day, can be spent in pleasurable activities to help you relax.

- **Focus is Key:**

So many times, you will find yourself tempted to do everything at once. This is an illusion. Keep in mind the fact that when you give everything your five percent instead of giving one thing your hundred percent, you start losing efficiency. You will never be able to focus on the task at hand because your mind will be jumping to the immediately next task.

Doing this will not only take your focus away from work completely, it will also give you added levels of stress and stress cannot only be cured by simple sleep.

Hence, if you find yourself with your focus deviating, consult the list you prepared in point one and start working on whatever comes first. No matter how pressing other tasks may seem, they can almost always wait. Plus, when you focus on one task, you complete it efficiently instead of letting all your tasks hanging, which will happen if you try and do everything all at once.

- **Make Room For Fun:**

There will be some tasks you enjoy doing so much that you would want to do them all the time. Now, that is not always possible but it is possible to do these tasks at least once a day. In your workday, include at least one task that gives you immense pleasure.

Be creative and you could actually include this in your work as well. For example, if you are a food-enthusiast. Turn a business meeting into a lunch meeting at your favorite restaurant. Similarly, if you have found golf to be your passion, hold golf-meetings to discuss business whilst having the pleasure of enjoying your favorite sport.

These tasks do not have to be over-the-top. If you look forward to listening to music whilst working, invest in a pair of headphones you can whip out whenever you find yourself working alone. Try and indulge in something that takes your mind off the mundane. Not every task and assignment will be as challenging and exciting as you want it to be. Indeed, these will make you feel like you aren't achieving to your full potential when that won't be true. Hence, to keep a positive outlook on life, have some fun while you work.

- **Respect Your Me-Time:**

Pick up any book on success and you will note that this is a point that all the greats have got down pat. If it is time to relax, relax you shall. For a certain amount of time a day, even if it is no more than an hour, set aside work completely. Clear your mind and focus on yourself. This doesn't mean spending an hour in front of the TV, though that may seem therapeutic to some.

For one hour a day, turn your phone to silent and relax. Take a long bath; pamper yourself. Indulge in some exercise or best of all: do yoga. Even by sitting in the lotus position, you will find that your muscles seem looser and your stress will gradually lessen over time. Whatever you do, do it consistently and no matter what, do not let work or anything else interfere in your 'me-time'. If you start working full-time, you will feel like a machine that hasn't been oiled in some time. You will feel strained and as if your brain is burning out. So, in order to avoid this, find some time to relax, even if just for the added productivity.

- **Step Back And See:**

Once in a while, put down your pen and step back and see yourself from an outsider's perspective. Make a list of all the bad habits you have. Poor sleep cycle, bad eating habits and poor exercise patterns might be a few of the major things you will find on your list.

Now, after each item, write the consequence of this habit. This practice is not meant to scare you and make you even more stressed, in fact, it will help you kick these habits. Like when you show a smoker the effects of smoking on the human body, this exercise is meant to show you what your seemingly harmless habits of carelessness are doing to your body.

Once you've made this list, you will find that every time you pick up something unhealthy to eat, you will be thinking twice. You will also find yourself making room for more sleep. Also, you will find that even if you can't devote hours to the gym, your body will try and remain active in other ways even if it means walking home from work instead of taking the bus.

- **Take A Vacation:**

This is an often-overlooked point when it comes to maintaining work-life balance. A manager, especially a young one, will believe that they are somewhat invincible and that nothing can hinder their performance. This is simply not true. Even though you might write off your own stress, your body is taking a major toll. This will affect your productivity and will cause you to slow down. As a result, your work will suffer majorly.

Hence, even if it means going away for no more than a weekend, take a vacation, turn off your cellphone, forget your laptop and relax. Try not to 'relax' by doing work-related activities because though you might be relaxing, you will be slacking off even at that. Instead, go swimming; maybe spend a day at the sauna, getting a massage to relax your inevitably sore and overworked muscles; or even just read a book in bed. Whatever you do, remember that just like your me-time, this time is meant to be for relaxing. So even if you would like nothing more than to catch up on sleep, indulge in an activity that you like enough to do it without the regret of wasting your time.

- **Communicate:**

Good communication skills are the key to any manager's success. However, work has a way of taking you away from the people who aren't immediately connected to work. Go through your cellphone's log and you'll only find a list of employees and business-related calls in the log.

Hence, hit up an old friend, talk to your family or your significant other. If you find that you don't want to talk to anyone like that, join a club. Visit a gym or even the park.

Even the simple act of talking is therapeutic in itself. You don't even have to talk about work. You will find that when you start talking, you will find yourself learning more about yourself than you knew before. Talk about hobbies; think about the things you would like to try someday. Talk to other people about their lives in order to learn about how they keep balance in their lives without burning out.

- **Set Boundaries and Respect Them:**
This is a crucial thing to do. With all the technology today, you will find that you will be bringing work home with you on more than one occasion, in fact, it will be expected of you to avail the opportunity to work more. However, as the idiom goes, all work and no play, similarly, when you find yourself working at three am, learn to set a boundary.

Make a timetable if it helps. Devote times to work and pleasure with some time for relaxation other than sleep. Don't be alarmed if you find yourself allocating more than eight hours of work. There is nothing wrong with wanting to work more. However, when that work begins to seep into your sleep and relaxation, even the time you eat, that is very alarming and unhealthy because it means that you are setting yourself down the path of destruction. Learn to set your boundaries and respect them like you would any other person's.

- **Find Your Crowd:**
If you find that you are still in need of some help, find other managers and discuss how you could help balance your work and life in such a way that nothing suffers. People who have been in the field longer than you will have a lot of insight to offer. Even a new manager might give you something to think about that you might not have thought about yourself. Hence, talk to other people about your problems and not only will they look more realistic to solve, you will also find an easy solution too.

Ross Elkins

Chapter 13

Common Management Mistakes and How to Deal With Them

To err is human and to forgive is divine. Hence, you shouldn't be too hard on yourself when you make mistakes. Unless you're one of those aliens walking around in disguise.

One way to keep you from being too hard on yourself is to look at mistakes as a great way to make progress. Think of Thomas Edison's attitude to his multitude of failed experiments on the light bulb: that they are merely ideas on what not to do for successfully making a working light bulb. Such an attitude will keep you from being discouraged and enable you to rise from the ashes of your mistakes.

However, when you go into the professional field you will find that you will not always be allowed to make mistakes. This is when you need help on how to avoid some pitfalls that might reflect on your career. If you are unsure of what to look out for, here is a list of common mistakes that managers make and how to avoid them:

- **Not Giving Feedback:**

  If you see a person crossing the street, looking at the opposite direction instead of where vehicles will immediately hit them and a speeding car from that direction about to hit that person, when will you yell at the person to inform of the pending danger: immediately, 10 seconds after or an hour after? Of course, immediately, which is when it's due! When it comes to becoming an effective manager, it's the same. You need to give important feedback when they're due.

  Never wait for the 'right' moment. If you see a team-member lacking in anything give them feedback on the spot. This might seem harsh but it will be much better than giving them a full performance review. It's always best to prevent bigger mistakes than curing them. This also gives you the opportunity to be kind and give people ample opportunity to learn.

- **Make Time:**

  Surely, your work is important. But as a leader it is important that you make time for your team as well. Sometimes it is better to take a few minutes off from your personal project in order to make time for your team. They will be both thankful and motivated that you care for them and their progress. This will also help them work harder so in the end you will benefit from the time you invested.

  People won't care about you unless they know you care about them and making time for the members of your team will go a long way towards making them feel that you do care for them. Chances are, they'll reciprocate with consistently good performance at work. Time is indeed gold and is a currency worth investing in, especially when it comes to your relationship with your team.

- **Stay On Top Of Things:**

One of the costliest mistakes you can ever make as a manager is to let a project fail under your watch. Nothing else speaks negatively of your ability to manage a team than this.

As such, don't just assign a project and go to sleep. This will cause a great deal of tension at the end of the day when the project is not up to specification. Keep a regular check on your employee so that you may tell them where they went wrong. Some employees might not like this but you will need to do it if you want a project to be completed the way you wanted it to be.

Remember, prevention is better than cure and by regularly monitoring a project's progress and how your team is implementing it, you'll be in the position to nip potential problems in the bud and ensure your project's success.

- **Don't Be Too Chummy:**

Too much of everything – even good things – is bad. Too much food leads to obesity and other health risks. Too much sleep makes a person lazy, unproductive and poor. Too much work makes a person sickly and poor because whatever material gains he or she may have had earned by working too much will be spent on expensive medical treatments. And being too friendly with your subordinates runs the risk of you losing their respect. This is because they will feel like they can get away with slacking and worse.

Hence be a boss and remember your place. Remember that at the end of the day your relationship is professional and you will suffer if you don't maintain it. Being a boss doesn't mean you have to be a jerk. Be friendly but not too friendly and be firm but not too tight that you suffocate people.

- **Maintain Clear Goals:**

Having vague goals is as good as not having any. What good are they if you don't know exactly what it is you want to accomplish? It's like trying to reach your business prospect's office in the next city using the map of the United States. It's too vague to be useful.

Define your goals and make sure you communicate it clearly to your employees. Don't be vague and don't base anything on a maybe. You are the boss and you decide hence make the decisions.

- **Not motivating:**

Different folks, different strokes. What works for one may not necessarily work for another. It's the same for motivation. Money is the strongest motivation for most people but a good boss knows that money isn't the only motivator. For many people, recognition, fame, being needed and seeing other people benefit are as strong motivations as money.

It's possible that your team will get motivated even if you just act politely and keep them happy. Remember to be as kind as you wish your bosses had been but remember to pull in the reigns whenever you feel the team going off track.

- **Don't hurry recruitment:**

  More doesn't necessarily mean better. In many cases, smarter means better.

  When it comes to great team performance, more members don't necessarily translate to improvement. It can actually pull performance down in some cases. When you have huge work load you will be tempted to delegate and hire more people. This can end up in loose ends and disaster.

  Take things slow and don't hurry a process that takes time. Consider the possibility of tweaking certain processes and job descriptions before rushing to hire more people. Recruit effectively, i.e. only when necessary, and not too much. If you need to, hire smarter and more efficient people.

- **Not Delegating:**

  Remember the example of Moses from an earlier chapter? Just like him in the beginning, you're only setting yourself up for disaster and stress if you fail to delegate well. Remember to divide your workload in an efficient way so that you get everything done while your team gets experience and no one get stressed out. Make the most out of your team – leverage on your team members' skills and expertise. You'll be glad you did.

- **Not Understanding Your Role:**

  If your role is unclear to you, you're like a car speeding down the wrong highway – you'll get nowhere fast. Actually, you'll get farther and farther away from your goal. Not clearly understanding your role can also be dangerous as you could be both abusing and misusing your power.

  Keep yourself aloof of employee duties but also remember that you are not a dictator. Remember, your job and do only what you need to do to get things done. Don't overstep your boundaries and to do that, you'll need to know what your boundaries are via your role.

- **Being Hypocritical:**

  Sometimes you will see a manager preaching something they cannot practice. This breaks the precious bond of trust between you and your team and it will also meant that you are assigning tasks that you cannot perform so your team will find it easy to ignore you in the future too.

  As discussed earlier, integrity is important if you want to become an effective manager. If you avoid the mistake of being hypocrital, you'll be able to continue enjoying the respect and commitment of your team members and continue being an effective manager who gets things done.

  Assign realistic tasks so that your team can realistically and consistently complete them without getting burned out or overworked. Remember to keep your team happy.

- **Failing To Get Your People Behind The Project:**

You're ability to effectively get things done as a manager is dependent on your people rallying behind you. Think of it this way – if you're racecar driver, your people are the engine – you won't get anywhere without them.

When you treat them poorly by acting all bossy, snotty and arrogant, you either discourage or anger them. Either way, you lose their support and if they leave you hanging in the air, you can kiss your managerial position goodbye.

Hence, never fail to bring everyone from the team on board and have him or her in your full confidence and vice versa. That shouldn't be very hard to do. A simple guideline is the golden rule: do unto them what you want done to you. You can't go wrong with that.

- **Assigning Tasks To The Wrong People:**

One of the ways you can accidentally prevent your people from having your back, even if they want to, is by assigning tasks to the wrong people. If you assign a task to a member of your team who doesn't have the necessary credentials, no amount of desire on that member's part to support you will ever make a difference.

This means do not assign tasks to people who are not qualified to perform them. If you assign a difficult task to a novice, they will either not do it at all or they will botch it up and give you a little-better-than-failed task. Both of these will be disastrous for your overall project. Hence, when assigning serious tasks, play every member to their strengths and assign people tasks they are qualified to do.

- **Failing To Anticipate:**

As a manager, make it a rule to anticipate the results of whatever task you are assigning. Have a result in your mind before embarking on any new journey. This will help you achieve a goal. Simply put, if you don't have a goal, what are you even working for?

Keep in mind that you don't have to anticipate each and every possible outcome of an assigned task. It is possible, however, to anticipate the major ones with enough critical thinking, evaluation and brainstorming. Hence, there's no excuse for you to make this mistake.

- **Ambiguity:**

  Many managers fail because they weren't able to clearly articulate to their members what they need to do and how to do them. Their team members, even though full of confidence, competence and commitment, fail miserably in trying to accomplish the team's goals because what they did wasn't in line with what was needed. The culprit? Ambiguity.

  Don't be afraid to ask your team for what you want or what is needed and clearly articulate it. It is of utmost importance that you tell them exactly what you need so that they know what they need to deliver to you. Remember that if you do not tell them what you have in mind, they will be unable to give you what it is that you need from a project. Hence, it is always a good idea to keep your team on track.

  Remember, no one ever got to an undefined destination. Keep your team members in the clear.

- **Changing Goals Quickly:**

  Rome wasn't built in a day. So is it with your team's goals – they need time to be successfully achieved. Once you have set a goal; be patient and wait for it to be completed. If you keep changing goals, you will leave projects unfinished and your team will always be on edge.

  In order to put them all on ease, you will have to be patient. If you find that hard to do, keep checking up on them in subtle ways and reminding them to speed up.

- **Being Too Aggressive:**

  Again, patience is a virtue, even when it comes to dealing with your staff. If you're too aggressive, you will offend them often and eventually, result in you alienating your team. They'll start hiding things from you, be it feedback or their problems.

  You can avoid this mistake simply by being courteous, respectful and polite. This doesn't mean you'll have to be a people-pleasing manager – may it never be! You simply have to watch your tone of voice and the words that you use, especially when correcting your team members. Never shout at them, even if you find it extremely hard not to. Don't even shout at them when they fail to meet a deadline since humans make errors often. Be soft and reprimand gently if you absolutely have to. Remember to not compromise on your principles but keep your team at ease so they work both with AND for you.

- **Having No System:**

Chaos and anarchy has no place in continuing and lasting success. When you manage your team off the fly, i.e., by gut feel alone sans any form of system, you run the risk of committing so many mistakes because you always try to do things differently and figuring them out along the way. With a system, you're able to do things – especially the recurring and repetitive ones – much faster and with less or minimal mistakes, if any.

Take for example delivering important documents to clients. If you don't implement delivery route system, you'll find your assigned members going back and fourth in the same area many times within the day instead of doing so just once or twice, which can save your organization a lot of time and gas money. Not only that, you're able to effectively carry out the delivery tasks and give excellent customer service.

The best way to do this is by sitting down your team and brainstorm. Identify your team's key activities and prioritize them accordingly.

- **Relying Too Much On Technology:**

  Yes, technology can help you increase productivity – but that's not an infinite benefit. Technology can certainly help you become even more productive, particularly in areas that don't require sound judgment and are pretty much predictable like generating invoices, summarizing data and formatting of reports. But things like content management, report writing and backing up of data in different types of media are still pretty much manual and can't be automated.

The solution is simple: don't. Backing up of data, for example, should be done not just by programming your computer to do so but also doing it manually via USB, burning in discs or backing up in an external drive and storing these media in secure places such as a vault or another offsite venue. If you rely on auto-back up and cloud computing, you're at the mercy of technology risks such as servers bogging down or lines being cut, which can prevent you from accessing the important data you backed up.

- **Undefined Success:**

What a waste of time and effort it would be to plan a trip, file for vacation leave days and stock up on supplies to go out of town for a much needed vacation only to find out at the time of departure that no one bothered to set a destination and make reservations. It's the same with being a manager. One of the biggest booboos that one can make is not defining clearly what success is. This is one area of conflict and tension between team members and managers because after all has been done, they couldn't agree as to the success or failure of an endeavor.

For example, I had an argument with a former boss when he asked me to consider a particular issue of the client in preparing my report. He didn't define what he actually meant by "consider". To me, it simply meant to factor the issue in my analysis and report writing but apparently, he meant it as prepare my final report around the issue. I had to work 2 more days on the report after I have already finalized it because he didn't define his idea of me successfully completing the report.

As a manager, ask yourself: what defines success to you? This is another reminder about having goals and having specific goals. Define success for yourself AND your team. Be very specific. Don't just consider "selling lots of our inventory" as success – define the number of units your team needs to sell to be objectively and definitely considered successful. Is it 10, 20 or 1,000 units? If you don't, you'll have an unresolvable issue of whether or not the team was successful or not.

Let them know what you want as a manager and where you want them to be as well. Confide in your team that you want them to be as successful as you yourself thrive to be. Engage with them and let them know that everyone's success depends on teamwork and if one party fails, everyone fails. Work together and take them into your confidence. You will notice that this will have a positive effect on your team and they will work harder and will offer you more productive results as well.

- **Not Giving Constructive Feedback:**

The ending point brings us full circle. Sometimes, managers might feel threatened by their employees. This will lead them to hold back on criticism that will ultimately result in a bit of tension in the short run and a lot of trouble in the long term.

One of the reasons for this is the wrong perception of what constitutes criticism and the wrong emphasis on the seemingly negative connotation of such. For many, any negative feedback or criticism is automatically bad and is perceived as an affront to a person's work or character.

Nothing can be farther from the truth. Criticism – also called constructive feedback – isn't about the person but about the results or methodologies. What makes such offensive is how it is delivered by the manager as well as the words used.

Realize that your team is your own tool and if you break your own tool or fail to keep them sharpened and ready, you are the only one who will suffer in the long run. As such, you'll need to give your team members constructive feedback as needed because only through such will they have the opportunity to grow personally and professionally, which will eventually give them the chance to get ahead in their careers. By denying your members the opportunity to receive such feedback, you're in effect denying them the chance to advance further in life.

Avoid making these mistakes by planning ahead and keeping track of how well you are performing. Remember, failing to plan is planning to fail. To the extent you're able to plan well and anticipate the situations that can lead to you committing these rookie mistakes is the extent that you can make the necessary preparations that will ensure that such situations don't happen or that their risks are minimized.

More than just planning, it's also important to monitor your performance as a manager and keep track of your progress or digress. Even the best-laid plans go to waste when there's no accurate and timely monitoring of actions and interim results of such actions. Monitoring and keeping track of your progress or digress allows you to continue doing the right things or stop doing the wrong ones and change course in order to get back on track.

Always remember to step back and see if you would consider yourself a good manager if you were working for yourself. If not, try and self-assess on how you could improve yourself. If you can't pinpoint your own problems discuss them with your team and your peers. Even approach your boss if you have to. Remember, you will have to work hard to be a good and effective manager so you will need to get all the feedback you can get and you will only get feedback if you give someone an opening to do so.

Conclusion

In response to globalization, rapid changes in external environments, and a desire by organizations to remain competitive, organizations have continued to flatten, decentralize, re-engineer their business processes, downsize, and empower their employees. To facilitate these changes and gain a competitive edge, managers are increasingly turning to team structures. Now you know how to tackle these situations in a much broader manner.

The actual team design used to support organizational goals may include such structures as cross functional teams, functional work teams, project teams, self-managed teams, intact work teams, employee participation teams, problem-solving teams, maintenance or support teams, and management teams. You can now pick up any strategy that is mentioned in this book and customize it as per your needs.

Unfortunately, the typical team-building effort proves ineffective, for three reasons. First, it relies on the services of an external consultant, who is often unfamiliar with the particular characteristics of the business, the organization, and its people. Second, it involves off-site activities in artificial settings that fail to adequately reflect actual work-site conditions and therefore make transfer difficult. Third, it fails to plan for, monitor, and assess the transfer of team-building activities to the work environment.

As per this book, the principal reason for the ineffectual outcomes of many team-building activities is the failure to use a critical team-building resource that is readily available in organizations — the manager. Managers play a critical role in maintaining a team climate through their day-to-day activities. For us, team building must be an ongoing activity internal to the organization.

As such, it should be made one of the manager's primary responsibilities, instead of the responsibility of an external team-building consultant or third party within the organization.

You are now aware that the following characteristics are required for effective team performance:

- Clear purpose
- Decision making based on consensus
- Shared leadership
- Listening to what others have to say
- Encouraging open communication
- Self-assessment
- Disagreement to certain extent
- Defining leadership style
- Networking
- Active participation
- Developing healthy relationships
- Role clarity
- Open mindedness and willingness to share
- Giving everyone working space

- Learning environment
- Providing all the necessary support as and when required
- Leadership style and management style

The golden nugget methods offer well thought strategies for today's managers to effective manage their teams and enable them to share their future. You will now be able to use any point from this book and just implement it at your work place with ease.

P.S. Continue your education on the next page...

Complete Your Business Relationship Skills Education With a Click Away:

Management: Golden Nugget Methods to Manage Effectively - Teams, Personnel Management, Management Skills, and Conflict Resolution

Communication: Golden Nugget Methods to Communicate Effectively - Interpersonal, Influence, Social Skills, Listening

Leadership: Elevate Yourself and Those Around You - Influence, Business Skills, Coaching, & Communication

Take Your Business Skills Further for Financial Freedom or Corporate Dominance:

Small Business: EXACT BLUEPRINT on How to Start a Business - Home Business, Entrepreneur, and Small Business Marketing

Marketing: Golden Nuggets to Market Effectively - Internet Marketing, E-Commerce, Advertising & Web Marketing

Sales: Foolproof Method to CRUSH Your Numbers - Selling, Sales Techniques, and Sales Strategy

Made in the USA
Middletown, DE
12 February 2016